ESSAYS AND POEMS,

WITH A BRIEF

AUTOBIOGRAPHICAL MEMOIR.

BY

J. A. LEATHERLAND,

Author of "Courtesy,"

ONE OF THE CASSELL PRIZE ESSAYS.

LONDON:
W. TWEEDIE, STRAND.
LEICESTER: PRINTED AND PUBLISHED BY J. WADDINGTON.
SOLD ALSO BY THE AUTHOR, AND BY W. DASH, J. TOLLER, AND T. WADDINGTON,
KETTERING, AND OTHER BOOKSELLERS.
MDCCCLXII.

"ON MAN, ON NATURE, AND ON HUMAN LIFE,
"MUSING IN SOLITUDE."

WORDSWORTH.

As a Pleasing Remembrance

OF THE HAPPINESS EXPERIENCED BY THE FAVOURABLE NOTICE

OF ONE

WHOSE ELOQUENCE HAS BEEN THE ADMIRATION

OF THOUSANDS,

AND WHOSE GOODNESS OF HEART IS EQUAL TO HIS HIGH

MENTAL ENDOWMENTS,

THIS VOLUME,

From the pen of an Invalid Artizan,

IS,

To SIR FITZROY KELLY, Q.C., M.P.,

(With his special permission)

MOST RESPECTFULLY DEDICATED,

BY

THE AUTHOR.

PREFACE.

THIS little Volume is submitted to the public with much diffidence. The prose pieces are altogether different from the light reading now so popular, and the author fears they may be thought too meagre and sketchy for the proper development of the grave topics discussed, his aim in writing them, being rather to furnish suggestive hints, than exhaustive reasonings. The conditions moreover under which most of them were penned were not such as to allow of any expansive treatment. The papers on "Household Economy," "Prose Fictions" and the "Immateriality of the Mind" are Prize Essays, and in their treatment the author was placed under restrictions as to length; and in dealing with the other topics, he was circumscribed in the same way by preparatory conditions. Should however these pencilled outlines be favourably received, he may perhaps fill up the picture at a future day, especially as regards the subject—to him a favorite one—of the Human Mind.

The gratifying notices which some of the papers have received from eminent literary men, and the call for a second edition of those which have been printed in a pamphlet form, have led the author to the present step of collecting most of his productions into a volume, in the hope that they may not be unacceptable.

The "Poems" (if they may be dignified with this epithet), are for the most part of a pensive character, and are the rough attempts of an artizan, to whom every advantage, except the most elementary instruction, has been denied. But he has taken Nature for his teacher; and although he may not have interpreted her with the same power or genius as other bards, he rests upon the hope that he may be considered a true disciple in their train. Upon Parnassus, there are tiny flowers as well as massive oaks, and all he covets is to be regarded as one of the lowliest upon the sacred mount—not a vagrant weed, that has no right to intrude upon its hallowed soil.

Some of the poems were composed very early in life, and bear marks of juvenile immaturity. For these and for the Volume generally, the author begs the candour and indulgence of his readers.

Kettering, June 2nd, 1862.

CONTENTS.

Autobiographical Memoir 1

ESSAYS:

Household Economy 43
Prose Fictions 65
Psyche 85
The Religious Element in Literature 109
Death 116
Common Sense *v.* Transubstantiation 122
Foreshadowings 126
The Uses of Poetry 133

POEMS:

The Dirge of Nature 139
Lyra Mortis 143
To Poverty 148
The People and Jupiter (a fable) 152
The Beautiful 154
The Standard of Truth 156
The World of Rest 158
On Seeing a Daisy Growing in November 159
Christmas 161
Thoughts in Spring 163
The Orphan's Dream 165
Birthday Verses 168
A Winter Piece 169

CONTENTS.

For a Sunday School Anniversary	171
Inscription for a Cemetery	173
The Prisoner of Eld	174
Wellington	177
Sonnet	178
Sonnet	179
Honour	179
Sonnet—To Mr. J. W. Dalby	180
Song	181
The Heart-stricken	182
The Forsaken Maid	184
Arcadia	186
To —— on the Receipt of a Lock of Hair	191
To ——	192
Stanzas	192
Epigram on &c.	193
Epigram—On a Bad Singer	194
Enigma	194
The Talisman	195
Lines to Earl Gray	196
On the Death of a Child	198
Reflections	199
The Praying Sailor	200
Honour	202
Spring	203
The Millers' Cottage	204
My Saviour	206

Autobiographical Memoir.

IT is with no self-complacent feelings that I sit down to pen this brief sketch of my lowly career. On the contrary, I review my past life with deep humility, and can only bring myself to the task of recording its history in the hope that it may prove instructive, as the experience of every human being must, if faithfully narrated. Providence has not seen fit to allow to any person the chance of living over again; but the history of those who have traversed a similar path—who have been elated by similar joys, and depressed by similar sorrows as their neighbours; who have substantially felt the same emotions, experienced the same griefs and cares, and committed the same errors as common humanity—in a measure serves the purpose to the young and inexperienced; showing them the blessed results of virtuous actions, and warning them to shun the breakers upon which others have been wrecked.

Auto-biography is also of service, as showing the varying force of circumstances upon different orders of mind—how, while one individual succumbs to them and sinks beneath their pressure, another with heroic vigour rises above them, and bends them to his will, or snaps asunder the bands, as Sampson the green withes that bound his sinewy limbs. It also reveals, as no other record can, the secret springs of action—the hidden, latent motives which spring up in the heart, and lead to conduct often enigmatical to the keenest and most diligent observer. But I must check my pen. I am not about to write an essay upon Auto-biography, but to furnish the reader with my own, which I will endeavour to do succintly and truthfully, begging his utmost candour in the perusal.

I was born at Kettering, on the 11th day of May, 1812—a dark day in the annals of England, noted for the assassination of the Hon. Spencer Percival, then Premier of England, and M.P. for Northampton. My father was a carpenter, but I remember little of him, for before I had completed my sixth year, he died, and I was left, with a younger sister, to the care of a widowed mother, who although in deep poverty, did her best to bring us up in comfort and respectability.

My mother was the daughter of a plain but good man, named Ayre, who, for upwards of fifty years, was a baptist minister, located first at Walgrave, then at Medbourn, and lastly at Braybrook. He was intimate with Carey, Andrew Fuller, and other worthies of the denomination, and was one of the twelve who met in a back parlour at Kettering, and founded the Baptist Mission.* He is also mentioned in Ryland's Life of Fuller, as having in the simplicity of his heart, asked

* See Ryland's Life of Andrew Fuller.

and obtained leave of the rector of Braybrook for Mr. Fuller to preach a funeral sermon in the parish church of that village on the death of one of his flock, the chapel being deemed too small for the occasion. The discourse was actually preached there, and if I mistake not, the courteous rector himself was present. I remember when a child, going frequently to Braybrook, with my mother, to visit my grandfather, and have more than once sat on a stool at his feet whilst he was engaged in conversation over a pipe with the celebrated Robert Hall. I have also a vivid impression of the pious and kindly old man leading me by the hand along the green meadows in the vicinity of the village, and teaching me that beautiful pastoral psalm, beginning "The Lord is my shepherd, I shall not want," which he illustrated by the scenery around. He was suddenly called from his work to his reward. Whilst engaged at prayer in the pulpit at an association meeting at East Langton, he sank down in an apoplectic fit, was carried out of the chapel, and never spoke again. His memoir may be found in the Baptist Magazine for May, 1826. I was a book-worm from my ealiest childhood, and it was a treat to me to ransack his dusty library, and pore over his ancient folios.

From almost infancy I was sent to a dame school, of which that pourtrayed by Shenstone is a model; but I do not remember learning the alphabet, or being puzzled by the awful hornbook. My mother also (blessed be her memory), taught me as only a mother can, and impressed upon my childhood those maxims of christian morals which are more valuable than an inheritance. She had a literary taste, and often used to please me with the rehearsal of those sweet little artless poems, which are the gems of our language. She moreover, read to me from Bunyan, Addison, Watts, Cowper, and others of our standard authors, noted for their simplicity, so that I early imbibed an æsthetic taste; and though circumstances denied me a classical education, I was enabled to drink at the "well of English undefiled."

I was, as I have said, from my childhood, passionately fond of books, and whenever I had a spare coin, off I used to run to the bookseller's shop for the tale of "Mother Hubbard," "Goody Twoshoes," "Little Red Riding Hood," and such-like lore. One day I bought a penny book, and being too impatient to wait until I got home, I began to peruse it in the street, and whilst so engaged, a puff of wind, to my no little vexation, blew it out of my hand into the kennel. Whilst I was weeping over its soiled pages, a gentleman passed me, and after enquiring what was the matter, gave me a sixpenny piece, telling me to dry up my tears and buy a better. Instantly my childish heart bounded with joy. I seized the proffered money, and ran to Mr. Dash's—whose windows were dearer to me than the pastry-cook's—and purchased a copy of a topographical work, called "Thirty-two Remarkable Places of Old England," with which I was amused for years. *The* book of my boyhood was, however, the "Pilgrim's Progress," a beautiful edition of which was given me by a paternal uncle. I used to read it from morning to night, and could not but believe the pilgrimage to be a real one, and often wished my mother to set out, with me and my sister, upon the journey. She endeavoured to explain that it set forth the pilgrimage through this world to a better; but I could not understand how it could be, and longed to visit the House Beautiful, and even to brave the lions, and the grim fangs of Apollyon. This book it was that early awakened my imaginative powers. A dream which my mother related to me about this time also strangely impressed me. It was in the year 1817, after two bad harvests. There was a great scarcity, and she told me how she dreamed that she saw Famine come into the house, a gaunt monster, holding up his lean, bony fingers, and staring with wolfish eyes!—how he tried to snatch the bread off the table; and how he howled, and howled until she awoke! The impression the relation of this dream made upon me I have never lost, and the reader will find that allusion is made to it in the Poem entitled "Poverty" at page 150 of this Volume. I was also much struck with many parts of the Bible. My favorite chapters were the xv. of the 1. Ep. of Corinthians; the xi. of Hebrews; Ezekial's vision; and most of the Apocalypse. These I used to read over and over again, but could not go on with the dry ceremonies of the Israelites recorded in Leviticus, or what appeared to me to be the barbarous slaughter of the Canaanites and Philistines; and to this day I have not read these portions of scripture consecutively. I also used to think the Epistles dry reading, but these are now my favourite parts of the Book of Inspiration.

In 1822, my mother married again, and I found myself one of a family of seven children. My father-in-law was a silkweaver; but as he was a kind of foreman or manager, he was somewhat better off than a common workman. Still with so large a family, both parents had enough to do, and my mother could not bestow upon me that care or attention she was wont. My stepfather was a strict disciplinarian, and a rigid Calvinist; and that austere and ascetic sect soon became very distasteful to me. I knew little of the joys of home, and was early called upon to provide for myself.

I had previously received a little instruction at a day school, kept by a Mr. S., who taught boys to write, spell, and cypher, for the sum of 6d. per week. The schoolmaster was not much of a scholar himself, but he did his best for us, and I respect his memory, as I believe he taught me for a considerable part of the time gratis, my mother being too poor to pay him. There I learnt the Rule of Three and Practice, but never dived into the mysteries of Fractions; neither were English Grammar or Geography taught in the school; I therefore fortunately escaped these regions of boredom. The severity of my schoolmaster's religious opinions, may be gathered from the following incident: In July, 1824, the corpse of the poet Byron passed through my native town, on its way to the village Church in Nottinghamshire where his ashes repose. Even then—young as I was—I felt an interest in the renowned bard, but possibly the gloomy grandeur of the funeral obsequies was the chief attraction. An awful storm heightened the sublimity of the scene. The lightnings flashed about the nodding plumes of the hearse, and the thunder cloud swept along in the track of the solemn procession—at intervals startling with loud peals the sable steeds that drew the bier, as though sounding a requiem for the departed, in keeping with the gloomy grandeur of his intellect and verse. In the pauses of the tempest there was a profound stillness, broken only by the monotonous tramp of the horses and the whispers of the crowd. On passing Mr. S——'s schoolroom, the door suddenly flew open, and his scholars thronged the little court which separated it from the street, eager to gratify their boyish curiosity with a view of the procession. I was not among the number, having then left the school, but was coming up with the spectators and within hearing. Instantly the master appeared at the heels of the truant lads, brandishing his rod, and shouting, as though he meant his voice to reach every one in the crowd, and attendants—"Come in boys, come in; he's gone to hell, he's gone to hell!" and driving his reluctant pupils back into the school he closed the door on the gloomy spectacle and disappeared.

In 1824, I was sent to learn the shoemaking craft, to which probably I should have been destined had not employment fallen off; but as trade was bad, I left it, and was placed in the loom under my father-in-law, where I continued until the spring of 1829, when I was apprenticed to Ribbon Weaving for five years. This was quite a mistake on the part of my parents. The master was only the proprietor of a branch factory in connexion with the Coventry trade, and none but the plainest goods were manufactured at it, so that I never had the opportunity of learning more than the commonest sort of work, made in refuse looms. I also had to compete with female workers, so that my earnings were very small. But this was not the worst: the factory was filled with the most ignorant and dissolute characters—tramps and immoral persons—many of whom had left the city, and had taken refuge here, because they were obliged to flee somewhere and hide their heads for a time. Had I twenty children, I would rather send them all to the workhouse, than to such a hot-bed of vice and immorality. What a place was this for an inexperienced lad like myself! It would have been a miracle had I left it unscathed. Happily however for me, the forms of vice by which I was surrounded were too low and gross to be attractive; indeed some of them were quite repulsive, and I was never seduced by them into any gross sin. I think too that I learnt something even from the dissolute characters with which I was associated. I saw human nature in more various phases, and became acquainted with some of the lowest forms of (civilized?) life, and thereby gained a kind of lore which is only to be attained by experience, and which I have since found to be useful.

One of the most sorrowful of scenes witnessed under the sun, is that of a sickly youth, worn down with pain and disease, wearily wending his way to a factory on a cold and dark winter's morning. This, many, many times, has been my lot; for, from my earliest days, I was a weakly boy, and suffered acutely from *calculi* in the bladder and kidneys. I have often felt in the morning as though I must have lain down on the factory steps and died; but a long day's work was before me, with the cruel taunts and jeers of my shopmates if I complained. I was, up to thirty-eight years of age, frequently afflicted with these torturing paroxysms; but strange to say, since a dangerous illness, which seized me in the autumn of 1850, I have scarcely had a symptom of this complaint. In my extreme youth, the malady was particularly painful, and whenever I did a harder day's work than usual, it was sure to bring on the complaint, so that from this cause, I could never get a shilling forward in the world, and was often in extreme indigence. Indeed up to the year just named, I had to grapple with three evils, each of them bad enough, viz., physical suffering, a failing trade, and extremely low wages.

I served my apprenticeship until twenty-one years old, and continued working for my master for about three years afterwards. I then left the ribbon factory and learned to weave velvet. Here I worked in a room with seven others—young men of quite different habits to my former shopmates. Gilbert's Map of the World hung at one end of the room, and entomological specimens adorned the window-sills. Here, instead of teasing and tormenting one another, all were affable and courteous, and each ardently bent on acquiring knowledge. It was like escaping from captivity to liberty—from Pandemonium to Paradise! Every one seemed so kindly disposed and so intelligent, that it was a pleasure to be among them; and I cannot help here mentioning the fact, that of those seven individuals, the six who survive, have with one exception, made their way in the world, and have attained a superior position to that of artisans.

I now devoted more time to literary pursuits, and passed my days very pleasantly with my intelligent shopmates. We clubbed together, and bought "Harris's Hermes," from which we gained some knowledge of the principles, elements, and philosophy of language generally, and of the English tongue in particular. We also formed the nucleus of a Mutual Instruction Society; arranged classes, and delivered lectures; and thus we both disseminated and received instruction. I have often blushed at my youthful complaisance and vanity in so early attempting to act the part of a professor; but whilst endeavouring to teach others, I was of necessity obliged to study the subjects myself, and in this way my crude and humble attempts became an important means of self-cultivation. As I never possessed in the slightest degree the power of extempore speaking, I was obliged to commit to paper the whole of my performances, which were therefore a kind of essays on the subjects I took in hand, and the writing of these trained me somewhat in the art of composition.

Some years before I made my *debût* as a lecturer, I had won some local celebrity as a versifier. I was passionately fond of poetry, being led to its study by accidentally meeting with Milton's minor poems, when about fourteen years of age. Though so young, I was instantly charmed with "Comus," and read it so much, that I could repeat it nearly all by heart. I still think it one of the most beautiful poems in the language, and deem it a pity it is not more generally appreciated.

My life in the days of my youth was a singular experience. In working hours at the Ribbon Factory, I mixed as I have told the reader, with the grossest society, and was the butt of my shopmates' ridicule, whilst of an evening, after working hours, I was petted in the parlours of some of the genteelest families in the town, and spent many pleasant hours in conversation by their fire-sides. Books were also at my command, as the libraries of these kind friends were ever open to me. In this way I studied many choice volumes, for, however oddly it may now seem, it is a fact, that for some years after I began eagerly to read, I could not obtain possession of but a very small number, and have often perused a volume over and over again, because I had no other to read, although at this time, I was hungering intensely after knowledge. Up to forty years old I never had half-a-dozen books I could call my own, nor did I possess an English Dictionary until about twelve months back, when I bought a second-hand copy of Johnson's miniature edition, without covers, for two-pence. I have sometimes thought this a fortunate circumstance, for had I possessed a good lexicon, I should have contented myself with referring to it, and should probably have soon forgotten the reference; but not having this help, when I have stumbled at a word which I could not spell or understand, I made it an invariable practice to search out its orthography or meaning, and have thus become better acquainted with it, and it has impressed itself upon the memory in consequence of the search made after it, just as a person will have a stronger recollection of a stranger he has taken the trouble to seek out, than of one whom he casually meets with. Lexicons are a kind of crutches or leading strings, but should not be made use of too often. It is far better to think out and search out a word or a subject, than to consult on every trivial occasion, a lexicon or a cyclopœdia. Still, of late I have found the inconvenience of having no books of reference, especially when writing against time, as I am often obliged to do.

I found velvet-weaving a highly suitable occupation for the exercise of thought and meditation—much more so than my former employment. In the ribbon loom, the worker has to manage a number of pieces at once, every one of which requires his care and attention; but in velvet weaving, the work is more under his command, and there is only one piece of work to superintend, and with good silk and use, the work becomes little more than mechanical, and affords scarcely any interruption to mental exercises. There is also far less noise attending the manufacture; and, owing to stopping every third time the shuttle is thrown across, to cut out the wire, the muscles are not kept in such constant motion. Some weavers of plain silk, place books before them to read whilst at work. I never could manage this with any good result. I think the secret of doing things well, is to do only one thing at a time. My plan therefore was to read at leisure intervals, and to ruminate on such reading whilst engaged in manual occupation. If in the course of my thoughts, anything struck me particularly, I made a note of it in a memorandum book, which I kept by the side of my loom for the purpose.

Such avocations as velvet weaving, are in my opinion, very favourable to self-culture—almost infinitely more so than the business of the trading classes; and if there is one study to which mechanical employment is particularly favourable, it is that of metaphysics. I think this is one reason why so many self-educated persons have pursued this study. The turn of such minds is also analytical, rather than synthetical. When the mind first awakens into activity, it attempts not so much to construct a system, as to search into first principles, and to trace existing nature backward to these first principles. And then again, what more natural than for the mind to study itself—to trace its origin and nature, and endeavour to track its destiny? The subject too may be studied with peculiar facility by the working man. No costly laboratory or apparatus is required; but the topic can at all times be followed up, without anything to interfere with the thinker, and without extraneous aid.

My reading at this time was desultory. I perused almost everything that came in my way. I was very fond of "Plutarch's Lives," Gibbon's and Robertson's Histories, the "Spectator," Dr. Johnson's writings, and Boswell's inimitable portrait of him; and I studied all the British Poets that fell in my way, from Chaucer to Byron. Periodical literature also engaged my attention. "Tait" I read and enjoyed for years—especially the articles contributed by De Quincy—and I was not a little proud on a poem of my own being admitted into its pages. From "Chambers's Journal," I gleaned much useful information, and it was a great treat when any stray numbers of "Blackwood," "Fraser," or the "Quarterly Review" came in my way. One of the latter, containing a capital account of Sir James Macintosh, as well as other brilliant articles, was a prize I once found on the counter of a grocer, and which I rescued from the ignominious fate of being torn up into butter papers. This I eagerly read, and afterwards studied for some years. "Blackwood" I more than once saved from a similar fate, perusing their contents again and again, enjoying a rich intellectual repast.

I have however conveyed an erroneous impression to the reader, if I have led him to suppose that I was a *gourmand* of books. Observation, meditation, and conversation, I regarded, and still regard, as necessary to the due cultivation of the mind. But I must not take any merit to myself, that I threw down my books, and mixed with the world, or retired to contemplate. The mere promptings of inclination led me thus to act, as is the case with thousands of others. Neither was I very particular as to the society in which I mingled, and I especially made it a point to study the manners and habits of the class to which I belonged.

Whilst pursuing my course of self-instruction, I was greatly assisted by gentlemen who kindly interested themselves in my welfare, among whom the late Rev. Henry Corrie, then curate, and afterwards rector of Kettering (brother to the first Bishop of Madras), deserves to be mentioned with grateful feelings. His extensive library was free to me, and he also kindly paid my subscription money for some years to the excellent town library at Kettering, and rendered me other favours. He once offered to get me into college. Had I accepted it, my whole after-life would probably have been different. I was also very generously instructed by a cousin of mine, who is now stationed at Oakham, as a Baptist minister. He started a manuscript magazine, to which I frequently contributed, and he never was happier than when improving the mental and moral condition of the youth of Kettering. Notwithstanding the extreme nature of his political sentiments, and some crotchety notions he held, I am persuaded that the town owes much to him for the pains he took in the instruction of its poor. He taught me a little Latin and French, and particularly pointed out the importance of tracing words to their roots, and becoming acquainted with the etymology of language, which I have since found to be a very useful and amusing study.

Another mentor whom I was fortunate enough to have at this time, was a young man named Goodman, not much older than myself, and quite as poor—by trade a wool-comber. Though he had no blue blood in his veins, he was one of Nature's aristocracy, being endowed with a prodigious intellect. When at the Sunday school, he had such a capacious memory, that he had learnt whole books of the Bible by heart, and I believe could repeat every hymn in Dr. Watts' hymn-book. I have known persons, in order to test him, open the book at random, and announce the first line, when my friend would take it up and repeat the hymn with precision, and with an emphasis and earnestness I have seldom witnessed. And his judgement, and mental powers generally, were equal to his memory. His mind was particularly biased towards metaphysics. Locke, Reid, Brown, Drew, and similar abstruse and acute authors, were his daily study; and when he differed from them—as he often did—he would maintain his opinion in as logical a manner as though he had been brought up at the feet of Aristotle. He was also fond of politics, but studied them as a science, not debating them with party heat and violence. Jeremy Bentham and Adam Smith were his guides. With their axioms he stored his mind, and from them he formed his system of political economy. Some of his opinions on these matters may be found in the columns of the *Northampton Herald,* his communications having been forwarded by the Rev. J. Litchfield, that gentleman being much pleased with him, and struck with his abilities, when on a visit to Kettering. Many a walk have I had with this young man, by night and by day, conversing the while upon philosophic topics; and I look upon the hours thus spent, as among the most interesting and instructive of my life. The whole of his survivors who knew him—and there were few of his townsmen who did not—can testify that I have not overrated his genius, and universal was the regret felt at his death. Reduced by want (for owing to the trade leaving the place, and being cut up by machinery, he could not obtain work), he was seized with a fever, to which he fell an easy victim; and although, as soon as his friends knew of his circumstances, help was poured in from all quarters, it was too late, and after a few days' illness, he died. The whole town mourned his decease, and crowds attended his funeral. Had he lived, I feel persuaded he would have distinguished himself. Such talents as he possessed, could not have remained long unrecognised.

In 1838, some gentlemen of Kettering offered prizes for the two best essays on the Best Means of Improving the Condition of the Working Classes. I tried my hand, and was fortunate enough to obtain the first prize, the adjudicators stating as the ground of their award, that they considered the one written by me the most practical treatise. The second was obtained by a fellow-workman, and has since been printed. This success cheered and encouraged me, and I determined to persevere in my literary studies. Another circumstance stimulated me still further. The late Earl Fitzwilliam, happening to hear something about the essays, did us the honour to request the loan of them for perusal. They were forwarded, and after a time returned, with a very complimentary letter, and the following Christmas his Lordship kindly sent me a generous token of his approval. This was highly encouraging. But the paper was a crude performance, and it contains several things to which I could not now subscribe. Its tone was too political—too revolutionary—and I have alluded to it, as affording an introduction to a period of my life that I look back upon with regret and remorse.

Chartism, then rampant, was the bane of my youth, and pierced me through with many sorrows. Not that I went to the extravagant lengths of many of my neighbours, for I never was a thorough-going Chartist*;

---

* This assertion may appear inconsistent with a Song that I penned, and which, inserted in the "Chartist Hymn-book," became very popular. But those who have studied human nature, know very well that in a time of popular excitement, the passions and feelings often act in advance of, and sometimes contrary to, the judgment of both individuals and nations. As the song cannot possibly do any harm now, and as it is perhaps the most spirited and energetic of my performances, I have determined to present it to the reader:—

> Base Oppressors, break your slumbers;
>   Listen to a Nation's cry;
> Hark! united, countless numbers
>   Swell the peal of agony!
> Lo! from Britain's sons and daughters,
>   In the depths of misery—
> Like the sound of many waters—
>   Comes the cry "we will be free!"
>
> Tyrants quail! the dawn is breaking—
>   Dawn of Freedom's glorious day;

but I was mixed up with a party who placed me in office among them, and made me their tool; and the time, money, and energies mis-spent—the excitement produced—the discontent engendered—the reputation damaged—the Utopian hopes raised and frustrated—the maddening disappointment experienced—the restless days and feverish nights constantly passed—made my life like a troubled sea, constantly casting up mire and dirt. And a circumstance that grew out of this connection entailed miseries upon me which I shudder to think of, and which calls for my readers' utmost pity, candour, and sympathy.

The Reform agitation had stirred society to its very

> Despots on their thrones are quaking;
>   Iron bands are giving way;
> Kingcraft, priestcraft, black oppression,
>   Cannot bear our scrutiny;—
> We have learnt this startling lesson—
>   "If we will we may be free!"
>
> By our own, our children's charter;
>   By the blood that fires our veins;
> By each truth-attesting martyr—
>   By their tears, and groans, and pains;
> By our rights, by Nature given;
>   By the voice of Liberty;—
> We proclaim before high heaven,
>   That we must, we will be free!
>
> Winds and waves the tidings carry;
>   Spirits, in your stormy car,
> Wing'd with lightnings, do not tarry;—
>   Bear the news to lands afar!
> Tell them—sound the thrilling story,
>   Louder than the thunder's glee—
> That a people, ripe for glory,
>   Are determined to be free!

depths, and caused political subjects to be freely canvassed among the people. As the trading classes had obtained the suffrage for themselves, it was but natural that working men should wish to possess it as well, and think themselves wronged by being excluded from voting for members of parliament. I was one of those who thought so, and I joined a society, which though at first it did not pledge itself to anything definite, afterwards became nothing less than a thorough-going Chartist Association—and a very notorious one it was. The Charter, and the Charter alone, was held to be the great panacea for the cure of every evil—social, moral, religious, and political. This flame was fanned by itinerant demagogues, who went about seeking whom they might devour—men who certainly possed the power of extemporizing with a vengeance, but who, making a market of the passions and feelings of the people, cared about the real interests of the nation, not one straw.

This society chose me its secretary; and as its leading men were my seniors—many of them persons whom I had long regarded with esteem, and had looked up to for teaching and guidance, my own minister being one of them—I thought I could not do wrong in accepting office. Indeed I esteemed it an honor ; and as my own intentions were honest, I gave others credit for honesty as well, and entered upon the duties without a thought or a dread of coming evil. I soon, however, found that I could not go to the extreme lengths of many of the fraternity, neither could I tolerate the chiefs whom they seemed so much to admire. The madman, O'Connor, and the fire-brand Stevens, in particular, I disowned from the very first, so that I was a perpetual drag-chain upon the society; but perhaps myself and two or three others were useful to it, by keeping it within bounds, and preserving it from the wild lengths to which it would otherwise have hastened. Whenever any one of our number seemed more violent than the rest, we used to get him on our acting committees. He then very soon found out the difference between saying and doing, and was generally sobered down into something like a practical man. I was soon convinced of the folly of political agitation, and grew sick of the wild projects of my associates. I saw that the dominancy of these associations would be equivalent to a reign of confusion; for the manner in which the bulk of the members were duped by their pseudo leaders, convinced me that they were not fit to be trusted with the franchise. I believe too, that our old and tried constitution, with such gradual expansion as the growing intelligence of the people may call for, is productive of more practical liberty than any that has ever existed, and I felt it then to be a duty I owed to society, to venerate and uphold it. I saw that it is easy to destroy, but difficult to construct, and harder still to establish. I was also disgusted with the conduct of many, who, arrogating to themselves the name of "Liberals" were the most illiberal of any. I saw that it was not liberty they wanted, so much as political power.

The perusal of Burke's "Reflections" at this time, also greatly modified my views, as did also, sometime afterwards, an expostulation, written by the Rev. T. H. Madge, rector of Kettering, and addressed to the society, and which, as its secretary, I was called upon to read to the body. My sentiments, therefore, gradually became quite opposed to those of its members generally, and after holding the office of secretary for more than four years, I felt it my duty to resign. I did so, and my resignation was accepted amidst a storm of hisses, mock cheers, and loud exclamations of "turn-coat," "weather-cock," and similar epithets, loudly vociferated. I well remember the wet and dismal night on which I was relieved of this, to me, onerous office. After I left the room, I hastened home; but my step-father, who regarded Radicalism with extreme dislike, had turned the key of the house upon me, as he had threatened to do if ever I attended these meetings again; and whilst standing in a gateway to escape the pelting rain—"this," thinks I to myself "comes of the policy of trimming. Here I am in a pretty predicament: kicked out of the Radical Association Room for not being a Chartist, and locked out of doors for being one!" However, I I scarcely know why, I continued to be a member of the society for some time afterwards. Perhaps the reason of my doing this, was to watch how it went on, and to mix in the debates, for I loved to place myself in opposition to the violent speeches and conduct of the body at large.

In the mean time, an event happened which entailed the most serious consequences, and filled me with mental anguish, and respecting which I know not to this hour whether I acted right or wrong. If, however, I have sinned, I have also keenly suffered, and would beg the utmost candour of the reader whilst I relate this sad affair.

The review of this part of my life fills me with dismay, and I am only supported under the weight of the reminiscence, by feeling that throughout the sad and embarrassing circumstance to which I am about to allude, I possessed a conscience void of offence, and that if I erred in judgement or feeling, I was swayed by the dictates of prudence, and acted as I thought for the best.

On the night of Saturday, the 23rd of February, 1839, I was from home rather late. I believe the town clock struck eleven as I was coming down the High Street on my way thither. Dr. Johnson—I think it is—says the events of a person's history often turn on very delicate pivots, and that his taking one street or another in a chance walk, which appears at the time of no importance whatever, may be of the greatest consequence through life. So it fell out with me on this eventful night. On reaching the end of the street, I could either have gone home by turning up Gold Street, or by taking Tanner's Lane. It appeared to me immaterial which, and after a moment's deliberation, I took the latter route. Near this lane, I met a man whom I knew, and had formerly worked with, whom I shall call Harry. He was coming from another cross road, and appeared the worse for drink, and I think would have slipped down, had I not caught him by the arm. I said to him "hallo Harry, where have you been?" "To the Bantam Cock," he replied. I said, "You appear to have been in the sunshine: I would advise you to go home." "Go up street with me" said he, "I have something to tell you;" and I turned back and led him towards his home. That same morning, a large rick of barley, standing near the town, belonging to farmer G—— had been consumed by fire, and Harry asked me if I had helped put it out. I told him I had. He said he had not, and had only heard of the fire that afternoon; "but," said he "I mean to be at more than one before long." I said "What do you mean?" "Why," said he, "there will be another fire in the town before morning." "You alarm me," I said, "how do you know what is to happen?" "O," said he, "I could tell you something, but if you split you'll be shot!" "Well what is it?" I asked, for my curiosity was excited. He said "There's a plan devised among the Chartists, to rise all over England this very night, and to burn the ricks down throughout the nation, and one will burst out not far from Mr. B———'s." He also told me they intended to shoot me for being a turncoat, and advised me to take care of myself. I replied "I hope you have nothing to do with it." He assured me he had not, but that he happened to hear of what was about to take place, and knew it to be true. I then made a stand, as if about to turn back and inform somebody, when he retracted all he had said, and told me there was no truth in it, but that he only meant to alarm me.

I have given the conversation as nearly as I can recollect it; but his admissions were made in such a broken way, and so incoherently, that probably my relation of it fails to convey a correct impression of it to the readers' mind. It was mixed up with dark inuendoes, and obscure hints; and though, after leaving him, the conversation impressed me, knowing that he was not sober at the time, I regarded it as a drunken tale, especially as he denied it before leaving me.

We parted, and I went home to bed, but not to sleep. The idea that something was about to happen, still troubled me; and I lay cogitating for about forty minutes, when I thought I heard the cry of "fire!" At first I supposed it was my own fancy, but in another second or two, cry upon cry, became awfully distinct. I instantly jumped out of bed, and went to the chamber window, where, in the direction Harry had named, the town was lit up with a lurid blaze, which my disturbed imagination magnified into a dreadful conflagration. Instantly flinging on my clothes, I left the house, and ran down the street in a state of phrensy, fully believing that a civil war had commenced, and fancying that the noises I heard were the reports of fire-arms. At that time, the most violent Chartists had been providing themselves with pikes, pistols, and ammunition; and I believed the day of their vengeance had arrived. On reaching the scene of the fire, which I found to be a rickyard—the very spot Harry had indicated—I saw two large wheat ricks in a blaze, with thatched houses almost contiguous. The most strenuous efforts were made to prevent the houses taking fire, and I fell in with a line of buckets, and worked as hard as I could to restrain the fury of the conflagration.

Fortunately, the damage was confined to the stacks; and, when it was somewhat subdued, I left my post to look round, and see if I could learn anything further, and especially if I could find Harry. I discovered him working away at an engine, apparently the most active and zealous of any; but when he saw me, he left, and we walked away together. I then entreated him to tell me all he knew. He said he would if I would go home with him, and I did so. As soon as we got inside the door, he locked it, put the key in his pocket, and told me I was in his power, and that unless I would solemnly swear not to divulge anything, he would take my life. I immediately saw my position. I was alone, in the hands of a desperate incendiary (his poor wife and children were asleep up stairs), and, being frightened, I made a dreadful vow that I would keep the matter an inviolable secret.

He then stated that what he had told me of the Chartist rising, was false; that he alone fired the stacks, with a piece of loose cotton, used in the weaving work, which he carried alight from home in his hat. He said he had been induced to commit the deed through reading the addresses of Stevens, in the "Northern Star," and that O'Conner's harangues had also greatly excited him. He said he knew nothing of the fire of the previous morning, but that it had suggested this to him. He also said that he intended to fire other rick-yards in different directions; but that after he had committed the horrid act, and had jumped the brook at the bottom of the hill, on looking back, his conscience smote him, and he returned to the fire by a circuitous route, and worked with all his might at the engine, to prevent its spreading. He then again implored me not to tell, saying, that on account of his being a Chartist, no mercy would be shown to him; he was sure he should be hanged; and for the sake of his wife and seven children, as well as his aged parents, he begged of me to keep the affair a secret. "Nay" said I "but you should have thought of them yourself, and not have done so wicked a deed, for their sakes, if not for your own." He said he was very sorry, and if I would keep the secret, he would lead a new life; but if I broke my promise, and divulged, he would deny all knowledge of the matter, or of ever telling me a word about it; and as no one had seen him do the deed, he believed my evidence would fail to convict him, and he should then say I had concocted the story for the purpose of getting the Chartists into disrepute. I felt the weight of this, and after giving him again my promise that I would say nothing, he unlocked the door and let me go.

I cannot describe my state of mind on leaving him, but I went home, and being weary, both in body and mind, I retired to bed. I remember I fell asleep; but the fiendish torch of the incendiary lit up the regions of dream-land, and the knife of the assassin appeared brandished over me in my fevered slumbers. On awaking in the morning, and calling to mind the events of the past night, I felt full of the most tumultuous anxieties. Sunday beamed, and the sweet bells chimed, but it shone no Sabbath-day to me, and I spent the greater part of it upon my bed, asking myself what was the line of duty I should pursue—whether I ought at once to go to the authorities of the town, and tell them all I knew, or whether I should preserve the secret inviolable. At first I thought of making a confidant of some one, and asking advice; but a little reflection showed me that this was impracticable. The nature of the secret was such, that had I imparted it to another, I should have placed him in the same predicament as myself. I was in a dreadful dilemma, which seemed to increase as days and weeks passed by. Two things especially weighed against my disclosing the secret. First the dreadful penalty of the law. It was then capital punishment, and I felt convinced this would be the culprit's doom if convicted. And I thought of his poor children being made orphans in this sad way, and of his aged parents' grey hairs being brought down with sorrow to the grave—for he was an only and well-beloved child. His father worked in the very next loom to me, and extremely bitter was he toward the unknown incendiary. He should have liked to see him burnt in the fire he said. "Ah," thought I, "poor old man, how little do you suppose it is your own son!" Then, on the other hand, I asked myself whether it was not an imperative duty I owed to society, to give up the culprit to justice, and risk all consequences; and whether, by concealing his guilt, I was not becoming myself an accessary, and an accomplice of the criminal. Had anything less than the punishment of death been likely to be awarded him, I should not have hesitated an instant, for my vow, forced as it was from me, I should have held as "violent and void," and the thought of his threat at times almost induced me to inform against him. I felt my life in danger, and I afterwards learned that for years he dogged my footsteps up and down, like the monster in "Frankenstein," and was often tempted to slay me for fear I should divulge.

The next week after the fire, large placards appeared, offering a reward, first of £300, then £400, finally of £500, from the government, to any one giving information which should lead to a conviction. These figures danced before my sight, like moons in troubled water. Not that I thought of taking the money. I would not have touched a shilling of it. I could not bear the idea of that. But the sight of the offered sum for a long time strangely affected me. The matter preyed upon my spirit in a most afflicting manner. I could neither work, eat, nor sleep. Books failed to attract me, and society was repulsive. Some times I was on the point of divulging all. At others, I resolved to bury the secret in my own breast.

Time, however, passed on, and when it was too late to disclose my secret, I felt somewhat relieved, especially as there appeared a reformation in the conduct of Harry. Soon after, I paid my addresses to a young woman,* to whom after a courtship of three years, I was married. But before we were united, I felt it my duty to disclose to her the circumstance I had so much at heart. For, thought I, should it by any means come to light, it would greatly surprise and afflict her, and I should not be dealing fairly with her by withholding that which might mar our connubial happiness. It is said that a woman cannot keep a secret, but my wife kept mine, though of course the disclosure filled her with surprise and alarm; and as the sequel will show, I acted judiciously in imparting it to her.

About a year and a half after our marriage—towards the close of the year—as I was at work at my loom, alone, in my own cottage, I was surprised by the sudden appearance of Harry. He seemed greatly agitated, and told me he wanted me. "What about?" I asked. "O," said he, "that old affair." "What," said I, "have you told anybody else?" "No," he replied, "not yet, but I soon shall. I want you to come with me." I

---

* A cousin of poor Goodman, the young man alluded to in the former part of this memoir.

replied, "I would have you seriously consider what you are doing. I cannot understand why you should wish to have it known now. Remember your wife and family!" He then burst into tears, and wrung his hands, saying, "I kindled the fire of hell that night within my bosom, and it has been burning, burning, ever since! I feel that if I tell I shall be easier, but if not, I shall go mad. I want you to go with me to the rector, or to some one else, and disclose all we know." Poor fellow! he looked the picture of remorse. I put on my hat and coat, and went with him to Mr. G——, at the bank, thinking it better to break the matter to him as I was well known to him. Harry waited outside, and I went in; but, thinking that he would probably repent of the step when too late, I made some excuse to Mr. G., and came out again, telling Harry the matter was still a secret, and if he pleased it should remain one. He, however, appeared more determined than ever, and wished me to go in again. I did so, but again came out without disclosing it; when, upon telling him a second time that it was still a secret, he exclaimed in an angry tone "Well, if you will not tell, I will," and immediately beckoned to a policeman, and gave himself into custody. I instantly ran home to inform my wife, who was in a delicate state, and I was afraid the consequences might be serious to her, but she was from home, and when she returned, seeing a police officer with me, she guessed the whole affair, was taken ill, and a miscarriage was the result, which confined her to her room for a month. The next day, I met Harry before a magistrate, when, to my great astonishment, he denied the whole of his previous confession, saying that if he made it, as the policeman and another witness, who was called to hear his statement, alleged, he could not have been in a sane state of mind. He was, however, committed to take his trial at the next assizes, and I was bound over to appear against him. What, moreover, was extremely vexing to me was, that some of his relatives wished me to retract what I had said; and when I told them I should not, they raised a story to the effect that I wished to extort money from him! This was my reward for all I had suffered on his account—for all my perplexity, sorrow, and anxiety!

At the trial, he pleaded "not guilty," and his friends employed counsel to defend him. But his confession to the policeman, sustained by another witness (Mr. W.), and corroborated as it was by my statement, was found strong enough to convict him. The learned counsel, as may be supposed, was hard upon me, but the judge (Baron Gurney) paid me a compliment, saying I had acted the part of a faithful friend to the prisoner; that it was doubtless a heavy trouble to me, and that I was not bound to reveal the offence; "for," said his lordship, "if everyone were to tell the secrets of their fellows, society could not exist at all." The rebuke of the counsellor did not affect me much, but this unexpected kindness of the judge overcame me, and I sunk down and relieved my long pent-up feelings by a flood of tears!

Little remains to relate of this sad tale. Whether Harry's repentance was genuine or not, he certainly acted a discreet part in reforming his life. His character, since his offence, had appeared so good, that several gentlemen of great influence appeared in court to speak on his behalf, and his lordship, considering the good character given him, and the length of time that had transpired since the committal of the crime, in a very touching address, sentenced him to a term of imprisonment for twelve months only. I may just add, that at the same assizes, another active member of our Chartist Association was also tried for arson, sentenced to transportation for life, and is now undergoing the horrors of Norfolk Island.

Thus my connection with the Kettering Chartist Association, rubbed off the bloom of my youth, and filled my heart with bitter remorse and regret.

The details of the above incident have occupied too much space to allow of more than a brief review of my after days. I shall therefore endeavour to be as concise as possible. After the Assizes, I began to breathe freely again, and, blest beyond many with an elasticity of spirits, they soon resumed their former tone, and for some time my life was comparatively smooth and pleasant. But in the winter of 1846—7, trade failed almost entirely, and myself and hundreds beside, were without employment. After seeking for other work in vain, I was glad to go back to my old trade of ribbon-weaving, but found little amendment in the manners of the weavers at the factory. The same reckless dissipation, coarse conversation, and wanton or brutal conduct, prevailed. One man alone, named B———, seemed to possess a kind of rough virtue. He was a gigantic fellow, and had a scar on his right eye—the result of an election riot at Coventry. He could neither read nor write, but prided himself upon his pugilistic skill, was a member of the ring, and had lately obtained the belt as the champion of Warwickshire. This man, however, had many good qualities. He always, magnanimously, took the side of the weak and injured, and would never allow them to be browbeaten or insulted, without acting as their protector. Had he been at the factory whilst I was an apprentice he would have defended me from many a brutal outrage inflicted by my ruffianly shopmates, the remembrance of which makes my blood boil. Those who are unacquainted with factory life can form but little idea of the cruel and brutal treatment, the systematic annoyances, the taunts, jeers, and blows, inflicted upon those that happen to be weaker than the rest, or do not choose to conform to the usages that prevail. To be singular is to be the butt of ridicule, and the object of petty tyranny or caprice, and immediately raises a nest of hornets around the unhappy victim, who take a fiendish delight in vexing and persecuting him. From these fellows B. many times protected me, invariably taking my part when he saw me wronged. He had a couple of fowls that laid eggs every day, and these eggs he used to give me for teaching him to read. Many a time has this sinewy giant seated himself by my side as docile as a child, whilst I pointed out his letters or taught him monosyllables. He seemed eager to learn, and in a few months could manage an easy biblical chapter, although at first he did not know one letter from another. He wished to learn to write, and offered to teach me to fight in exchange. I gave him a few caligraphic lessons, but declined his instructions in the noble art of self-defence—though, had I met with him a few years earlier, possibly I might have availed myself of his offer, and gone through a secret training that I might unawares have been even with my tormentors, and repaid them in their own coin. I am sure they would have been as pusillanimous as tyrannical.

After a short time, the weaving failed in all its departments, and I was entirely thrown out of work. I had no resourses, and the workhouse stared me in the face. Many of my shopmates with their families took refuge in it, and I must have done so too, but for an experiment I made in common with two or three others. We could not get work as journeymen, so we turned manufacturers. A few pounds sufficed to purchase a little silk, which we made up into plain and fancy vests —at that time much worn. The scheme in a measure succeeded, and for about three years, both myself and wife were engaged in making them, and when we got together a little stock, I used to vend them in the towns and villages in the vicinity of Kettering. In this way, I visited every town within a circuit of thirty miles, and lingered with peculiar pleasure in places celebrated in local or national history. In my peregrinations, I trod the cloisters of Peterborough, and the ruins of Fotheringay; visited the heights of Naseby, and the classic banks of the Ouse; entered the house where Cowper lived at Olney, and lingered in the golden autumn, amid the sweet scenes of his daily walks.

I continued this alternate manufacturing and travelling, until July, 1850, when a serious accident brought my wanderings to a close. This untoward event completely upset my schemes, and nearly cost me my life. Never did I feel in better health or spirits, than during my last journey in this capacity. A high and narrow omnibus ran between Northampton and Kettering, on the top of which I one day took my seat. The weather was pleasant, and all went on well, until we were about to enter Northampton, when one of the wheels spun off the axle, and the carriage upset. I fell on my right side and narrowly escaped being crushed by the vehicle and its heavy luggage, but I managed to get up, and to go to the assistance of the inside passengers, all of whom were females. Before the day was over, I began to feel that I was severely injured in the right side. I was seized with a strange pain, accompanied with a swelling, and reached home on foot the next day with the greatest difficulty. For some weeks I kept getting worse, but still went about. After a time, however, I was obliged to keep my bed altogether, and my surgeon informed me that a tumour was gathering, which he attributed to the accident proximately, though he thought the seeds of the disease had been long latent in the system. This tumour began to enlarge, notwithstanding every effort made to send it back or to disperse it, until it reached an enormous size—the largest my surgeon said he had ever witnessed in a living subject. In a short time I was a most pitiable object, and the faculty held out no hopes of my recovery. I lost the use of my legs entirely for many weeks, and for three months I was unable to turn myself in bed. In the spring of 1851, the force of my disease somewhat abated, so that I was able to get up, and even to walk about a little, but was often in great pain, neither had the swelling much diminished.

In this chronic state, the disease continued until the commencement of 1852, when I was suddenly seized with the most excruciating pains I ever experienced, and became so alarmingly ill, that my dissolution was hourly expected. What added to my affliction, was the state of my mother, who had, since the death of her husband, come to reside under my roof, and was now dying in the next room. She expired on the 22nd of January, but I never saw her after the 6th, being unable to leave my bed. About this time, my tumour broke inwardly and for several weeks caused a great prostration. This was the crisis of my disorder. My afflicted wife nursed me with the greatest care, and I felt that under Providence, my life was saved by her unwearied assiduity and attention. My infant daughter too, born in February, 1849, greatly cheered me with her innocent prattle, and I shall not soon forget the glee with which she clapped her little hands one morning when she heard the sound of my voice after I had been unable to speak for some weeks. After the tumour had discharged itself, I began sensibly to mend, and by the following June, was sufficiently recovered to be able to take a walk. People who had seen me in the worst, looked upon my convalescence as litttle less than miraculous, and I felt indeed as one alive from the dead. O, how sweet did the balmy airs of spring play around me, and how glorious were its sunny skies, after the long and dreary confinement I had undergone! The thrill of pleasurable sensation experienced, seemed to compensate for the suffering endured, suggesting the thought that perhaps the natural evils to which all are more or less doomed in this world, are meant only to enhance the appreciation and intensity of the bliss in that angelic state when "sorrow and sighing shall for ever flee away!"

Since that time, my health has been such as to allow of my getting a somewhat precarious livelihood; but my constitution had received too great a shock to admit of more than a partial recovery. I have been quite incapable of manual labour, but Providence has not left me and my family to want, and indeed has cut out a path for me in a way I never anticipated.

When, in my youthful days, I took up my pen for amusement or self-instruction, I little thought of being able to live by its exercise. But so it has turned out, and that in a manner highly suitable to me. I am not confined to the drudgery of a desk, which would indeed be beyond my strength, but my calling being alternately one of gentle exercise and a few hours' writing, is just what is suited to my state, and what I am fond of. It is true the remuneration is but small; but I have no desire to live in any other than a plain humble way, and it affords me—what I enjoy better than any worldly luxuries—" divine leisure," as Charles Lamb designates it, and the opportunity of indulging my taste for reading and study.

In May, 1849, I was engaged as local reporter to the *Northampton Herald*; and although for some weeks, during the intensity of my affliction, I was compelled to discharge the duties of the situation by proxy, I still retained it—the members of the sick-club to which I belonged, kindly allowing me to forward the news (which my wife and others collected), merely deducting three-pence from my weekly pay, as an acknowledgement. Many a time have I sat pillowed up in bed, writing dispatches, until the pen has dropped from my fingers from sheer exhaustion.

It is highly comforting to me to think that throughout this long and heavy illness, I never once had occasion to apply to the parish for relief, and that as soon as possible, I flung myself off the club funds.

About this time, I succeeded in being placed on the staff of other local newspapers, with which I am still connected ; and the salary I draw from them, together with what casual writing I can get, makes up my small income.

I have, within the past few years, succeeded in obtaining five prizes, in small sums of money, for Essays, three of which are contained in this Volume, one I have omitted, and the fifth, being copyright, I am not able to publish. It is printed in the volume of Essays, written by working men, published by Mr. John Cassell in 1861. These brief papers have been of much service to me. The sums awarded, I need not say, did me great good, and the competition itself cheered me on and stimulated me to perseverance. The Essays also brought me several kind friends, who have generously assisted me, when under the pressure of pecuniary difficulties ; and in many ways have helped me in my struggles. Indeed all through my affliction, the kindness of several persons —some of whom were but slightly known to me—has been such as calls for the livliest expressions of gratitude, and they have my warmest and most sincere thanks.

In the spring of 1859 a great disappointment befel me, which, though I felt much at the time, I have reason to believe Providence overruled for the best. Through the kindness of our two county members, Lord Burghley and G. W. Hunt, Esq., I obtained the office of postmaster of Higham Ferrers, then vacant, and went to that town in the confident expectation of being initiated in its duties by a clerk from the General Post Office, by whom I was apprized of the appointment in my favour. When there, however, I soon discovered that the party residing at the old office would not resign the house to me, although offered the most liberal terms; and the town was so densely populated, that after using strenuous exertions, I was unable to obtain a place sufficiently commodious for the business. To my great vexation and regret, therefore, after the lapse of some weeks, the Postmaster-General annulled my appointment, and gave the situation to a tradesman of the town, who was residing in eligible premises, at the same time informing me that this was the only ground upon which it was taken away—that he had not the slightest personal objection to me, but on the contrary he believed I should have made an efficient postmaster.* I cannot, however, help thinking that the Government should provide its office in every town, in order to insure the carrying out of this important branch of the public service, independent of any contingency that may arise, and to prevent conferring an impracticable situation upon any one, thereby entailing expense and disappointment, where a benefit is intended. I was some pounds out of pocket by this mishap, to say nothing of the suspense and anxiety it occasioned. Still I think the loss of the situation turned out for the best, as soon afterwards a disease fell in my legs, from which I am still suffering, and this would

* The above is the substance of letters received from the General Post office, in March and April, 1859, and which I have still in my possession.

have prevented my delivering the letters, which, at Higham, is done by the post-master, and is an important item in the stipend.

And now, courteous reader, I would conclude by introducing to you the slight efforts of my humble pen, which are presented to your notice in this little volume. It opens with the discussion of a subject of great practical importance to the poor man*—a subject which I regret I did not study more in my youthful days, but which on that very account I am perhaps better able to treat of than if I knew nothing of the evils which arise from its neglect. Like poor Gloucester, when his eyes were plucked out, I "see them feelingly." There are none so well able to speak of the mire and clay, as those who have been in the pit, and I have fathomed its lowest depths. Mine, therefore, on this subject, are words of experience, and I hope they may be found of service to others, even if in some measure they condemn myself. The other topics treated upon are for the most part of a more speculative kind, and need no special remark here. Many of the compositions were written amid noise and bustle—in an apartment common to a whole family, or the din of a workshop—and therefore, whatever inaccuracies of grammar, or ungracefulness of style may be observed in them, will I trust, be pardoned. Their composition has greatly cheered and enlivened me amid sickness and sorrow, toil and obscurity, and I would fain hope that their perusal may not be altogether unpleasant or unprofitable to the general public.

* "Household Economy," one of the *Dial* prize Essays, and published in that newspaper.

ESSAYS.

The Household Economy of the Workman.

A WORKING-MAN is simply a man who works. This assertion may appear a truism, but it is often lost sight of or ignored in real life. The glory and excellency of his manhood is sometimes sullied by his own ignorance and vices, or forbidding habits; at others it is hidden by the menial or coarse nature of his employment—in which case he is to be pitied; and again it is often unrecognised, owing to the supercilious pride of those above him in the social scale. Be this as it may, however, abstractedly considered, he is neither worse nor better than others, and it will generally be found that in proportion to the degree in which he respects himself and those about him, and fulfils the duties of his station, he will be looked upon and respected by all whose esteem is worth possessing.

There is nothing which more commands this recognition, or is more essential to a working man's comfort and respectability, than Household Economy. Its importance ought to be impressed upon his mind in early life, and be made a study, a science; for if he be ignorant of, or neglect its maxims, he will dearly rue it with every passing year. His house is, in a sense, a part of himself, and reflects his character accordingly; and the name which he generally bears, that of husband or "*house band*," should remind him that he is the *band* or *bond* of the house, viz., he who should bind and hold it together. The difference between good and bad housekeeping is so obvious and striking, that I need only point to different families in every town and village for its practical exemplification. In one dwelling, all is order, neatness, and comfort. The exterior of the cottage has an air of cheerfulness which is refreshing; and we have only to open the door to see a picture of tidiness, if not of elegance. The different articles of furniture, though homely, are well arranged, and in their proper places. The walls and the floor are clean, and the hearth well swept. Perhaps a smiling housewife invites us. If so, ten to one she is busy with her needle, except indeed we find her in the forenoon engaged in culinary operations. There is also in such houses an air of quiet and repose, which is very pleasing. I have often been struck with the absence of bustle, noise, and hurry, as if the household work were done by fairy fingers, we cannot tell when. Such a trait constitutes the working man's home, and is the very perfection of comfort. In another dwelling hard by, how different the scene which presents itself! Dirt, squalor, and want, meet the eye both within and without—broken panes mended with paper, or stuffed with rags; threshold and floor grim with filth; mouldy, ill-washed clothes lying littered about in corners, or on chairs and tables; the hearth glutted with ashes, potato-parings, and onion-peel; the paper on the grim walls torn and hanging in shreds; in the passage, a dirty bucket or washing tray, placed there as if on purpose for the visitor to break his shins against; a treacherous creaking staircase leading to a real "chamber of horrors," where the wonder is that any one can win repose for a single night. Such is the difference, by no means overdrawn, presented by thousands of working men's homes in England; the one pleasant abodes of comfort, health, and prosperity; the other cheerless squalid tenements, where fevers lurk and foul diseases are generated—dreary uncomfortable places, which the stranger shudders to enter, and from which the working man is glad to escape, though it be to the tavern or the skittle-ground.

And if we glance at the circumstances of the different inmates of these houses, we shall generally find them correspond with the character of each. The inmates of the clean and tidy dwelling are beforehand folk, who can pay for their purchases when made, and have a little in reserve for a rainy day; or, if they live from hand to mouth, they take care to make both ends meet, not involving themselves in debt and embarrassment. Those inhabiting the dirty tenement, on the contrary, are poor and miserable; are constant attendants at the pawnbroker's shop, and beset with duns and County-court bailiffs. And yet the joint earnings of the latter family are fully as much as those of the former. The difference lies in the manner of expending them; in the managment of their respective household affairs; in tact and method, or the want of them;—in short, in the observance or neglect of that eminently practical virtue *Economy*. I am aware that there are numerous special exceptions to the above representation. Many families worthily striving to obtain things honest in the sight of all men, seem doomed all their days to struggle against wind and tide—misfortune in some shape or other is constantly besetting them, until they are ready to lose heart and sink under the burden; while others seem to prosper, do what they may—people to whom good luck stands in the stead of virtue and endeavour. There are also innumerable incidents that mix with, and give a colour to, the circumstances of all, independent of their own exertions, so that the picture which I have endeavoured to sketch of the two diverse families must be received with some reservation. Still, I contend it is the rule, and may be seen exemplified in every town and hamlet of Britain. Let us then briefly note down and reduce to system, the prime axioms of this important part of practical knowledge—important surely to all classes, but doubly so to the man who has to earn a livelihood for himself and those dependent upon him, by the sweat of his brow; whom sickness and misfortune may at any time invade and deprive of the power or the means of earning his accustomed bread, and cut off all his resources.

A boy in a Sunday school known to the writer, was once asked by the teacher, what economy meant. He replied, "paring potatoes thin." The answer was received with a smile, but I contend that the definition was right as far as it went. The lad had got a just idea of the matter. His rule only wanted carrying out, and applying to things generally, to be perfect. Economy may probably be defined to mean the careful and proper use of whatever is taken in hand; and household economy the careful use of goods, time, and money; or in other words, turning them to the best advantage. To do this, requires habits of forethought, prudence, self-denial, frugality, industry, honesty, order, and a careful attention to little things. Economy presupposes morality, for there is not a vice but what is more or less expensive, and therefore to indulge in any one is in direct opposition to the maxims of economy. How costly, for instance, is the vice of drunkenness! Not only does the money expended in drink in the course of a few years tell up to a large sum, but there is the time worse than wasted, the physical energies weakened, the character damaged, the intellect enfeebled, the grosser passions fostered and stimulated, the affections deadened, the heart hardened, the family neglected. And so of pride, lasciviousness, etc., there is not one of them but deducts from the family exchequer, and is therefore inconsistent with, nay, totally opposed to, the practice of household economy. We suppose, then, morality to prevail in the household, and proceed to enquire what are the principles which must be constantly acted upon in order to carry out this important duty?

First, then, I would mention, as of primary importance, *Order* and *Method*. I have classed these together because I consider them as but different manifestations of the same principle; or, to speak correctly, method is but the carrying out into every-day practice and observance, orderly regulations. This is often regarded by the young as an irksome task. Their constitutional buoyancy spurns set rules, and they pant to act according to the promptings of their caprices, and imagine they show a noble magnanimity in disregarding the plodding, systematic way of living which their seniors recommend. But in this, as in many other things, "it is good that a man should bear the yoke in his youth." And when he takes to himself a wife, and becomes the head of the household, the carrying out and enforcement of Order and Method in his affairs will be found of prime importance; and what, perchance, he at first found a wearisome and galling task, will, if persisted in, become in time a positive pleasure and a source of satisfaction. How comfortable must be the reflection to a well-regulated mind, that his affairs are under his own supervision, and that, having confidence in his wife, he is able to manage them as a skilful mechanist regulates a machine. In order to do this, the entry of his transactions, as well as of events generally, in a common-place diary, will be found useful, not only from the assistance the record will render him, but also because it will tend to foster habits of regularity.* I would also recommend the keeping of a debtor and creditor account, in a small ledger, and its careful perusal at stated intervals. It would save him many an anxious hour. He would know at once how he was getting on, and would

---

* Keeping a short diary will be found of great service as a help to the memory. Without it, past circumstances will soon present themselves in a confused mass, so that it will be difficult to tell when any given event took place. But by this method, though the precise fact may not be noted, the association of ideas will soon call it up, and give the individual an opportunity of enjoying life afresh, and will in a sense renew it. And how sweet at times thus to chew the cud of bygone days! How fair do they seem in the retrospect! Memory no less than Hope paints a magic scene, "clad in colours of the air," whilst in the words of the same sweet poet:—

"The present's still a cloudy day,
Still plod we on the same coarse way."
Dyer's Grongar Hill.

have the chance of regulating his affairs accordingly. His maxim, then, should be, "A place for everything, and everything in its place." He should also learn to methodise his time. Duties, as much as possible, should be performed at stated seasons; the observance of which will tend to cherish habits of punctuality. I hope the few hints thrown out upon this topic may be of use, as I am persuaded that without the careful study and practice of the virtues now recommended, Household Economy can be but very imperfectly carried out.

Secondly. *Avoid incurring debts.* The law is perhaps harder upon the poor debtor than upon insolvent traders. Unfairly so, it appears to me. But I imagine the theory is, that a working man has no right to incur debts. Supposing his resources fail, owing to ill health, or want of employment. If he get into debt, it must generally be without a fair and reasonable expectation of discharging the obligation; since, if his income yielded him a surplus above his weekly expenditure he might be living upon that, and need not go into debt at all; whereas, if these wages were only sufficient, in times when things went smoothly with him, just to keep the wolf from the door, how is he to recover himself, unless he can see that his misfortunes will terminate at a given period, and that either his wages will increase, or the price of food and clothing diminish in a ratio which will enable him to meet his engagements?—contingencies which he has no right to calculate upon. I am aware that this may be regarded as a hard saying; but there is nothing more uncompromising, unpalatable, and stern, than Truth under certain circumstances; but it is better to look it manfully in the face than to shirk it, since by doing the latter we shall only resemble the hunted ostrich, which is said to hide its head in the sand to escape its pursuers. Hope, I know, tells a flattering tale, and probably the greater part of those miserably in debt, imagine that they shall be able to meet it at a future day; but the wretchedly embarrassed state of thousands of working men sufficiently proves that the debtor has built upon the sand, and is sinking lower and lower in penury, want, and obligations, from which at the present time there is no honourable escape. It should be remembered that debt increases debt. Like a snow-ball on the side of a mountain, it is small at first, but accumulates by its own action until it forms an avalanche which is fraught with destruction. Another important thing which should be borne in mind is that there is no such thing as borrowing one's-self out of debt; but that the very effort of obtaining temporary assistance in many cases only increases the standing burden. Money is sometimes granted at an enormous rate of interest to working-men. Of course few could pay this, time after time, without being ruined, and the consequence has been a County-court summons, a distress, and in many instances a prison. I need not say that distress, wide-spread and calamitious, has resulted from such a pernicious system —distress which is still on the increase, and which if not checked by legislative interference, will increase the poors-rates to an enormous extent, and involve the middle class as well as the lower in its melancholy consequences. A prime axiom in household economy is to endeavour to have an equivalent for money paid; but if a working man runs in debt, he very rarely gets value for his money. In some villages it is a recognised custom for the baker and the butcher to make a charge for the trouble of "setting down." Thus, if the market price of flour be 2s. 6d. per stone, the baker will book it at 2s. 8d.; and if the regular price of meat be $6\frac{1}{2}$d. per ℔., the butcher will take an account of it at 7d. And then, persons in debt at a shop are, as a consequence, tied down to it. They are not free to purchase a good article if they see it elsewhere, are often put off with the rejected commodities of the ready-money customers, and treated with insolence and affront as well. O, how sweet is the independence of entering a shop and knowing that you have the money in your pocket to pay for the purchases you intend to make! With what blandness and courtesy does the dealer receive you, while it may be, the poor creature who is "in his books," though first at the counter, has to stand by and give place to you, happy if he escape the affront of being talked *at*, and insulted by inuendoes, whilst you are waited upon, although he has traded at the shop for years, and paid over scores of pounds. One of the worst ways of contracting debts is by resorting to the "tally system" as it is called, *i. e.*, taking goods of travelling pedlars and paying for them by instalments, almost always, as may be supposed, at exorbitant prices. The system has in many places become a public nuisance, especially in the villages. Thousands of these fellows, roaming throughout the length and breadth of the land, continually haunt the cottages of the peasantry with the most unblushing effrontery; intruding upon the privacy of families, and watching the opportunity to spread their tempting wares—often gay and gaudy apparel—before the wife, in the absence of her husband. And what female heart can resist the temptation? This often leads to family quarrels. I have known more than one household broken up on this account. And many are ruined by paying an extravagant price for goods they could have done without, and sometimes even worse consequences follow. The wife, it may be, is enticed to break her marriage vows by the intrigues of pedlars; or the daughters are seduced, and family happiness wrecked and destroyed. I believe there is a vast amount of immorality occasioned by the solicitations of these itinerant traders. I have heard them brag of it; and after having paid particular attention to their doings for years, I hesitate not to say that on the ground of morality as well as economy, the practice ought to be discountenanced by every one who regards the interests of the poor.

To those who are about to start in housekeeping, I would recommend, as the best means of avoiding debt, the steady saving of a little money to commence with. There is a great deal more than the arithmetical difference between having five pounds upstairs and being five behind hand. The former is by far more than ten pounds the better man. The one has a clear start, the other is embarrassed; the one can make the best of his money and replenish or increase the amount by his weekly earnings, the other is obliged to seek for credit and take just such goods as are offered him without expostulation; the one has his mind at rest, and the other is filled with anxiety; the one is going right, and the other going wrong; the one starts in the way of pleasantness and comfort, the other in the downhill path of sorrow and woe. Better, far better, to wait until this can be done, even if wedlock be delayed for years, than to rush into the matrimonial bonds without forethought and without means. We will suppose, then, a clear start; a perfect loveable understanding between man and wife, and a clean, commodious cottage with plenty of sunshine about it. A couple may then, with ordinary prudence, keep out of debt, and so manage, that at the end of every passing week they will be richer than at the beginning. A year passes by and a little stranger comes to be loved and cared for. This event should be anticipated, and due provision made for it, and if the husband's earnings will not admit of the way of living being kept up, necessary retrenchment should be willingly and cheerfully made in time. It will be found a far easier matter to economise at the outset of life than at a later period. Habits are very stubborn, and not easily subdued, and if indulged in, soon degenerate into vices. It is also much better to rise than to sink, and, therefore, care should be taken to commence low enough. No wholesome gratification need be dispensed with to accomplish this. Our natural wants are but few; it is the artificial that are the most expensive.

The easy, insidious way in which debts are commonly contracted, renders caution the more necessary. A family sometimes thinks no more of fetching goods from a shop than water from the pump. Is a pail of water wanted, the well is there ready to supply it. Is a pound of sugar or currants desirable, the shop is but at the street corner, and the goods are forthcoming; whereas, if the ready money had to be raised and told down upon the counter, the purchase would be pondered over, and in many instances the question would be asked, Cannot I do without this? For after all, it is not absolutely necessary, and I shall have hard work to eke out my income until the week's end. This facility of credit therefore leads to extravagance and to embarrassment; for, although a long credit may be given, a reckoning-day will come, when the debtor will probably stand aghast at the fatal score which he is unable to pay, and become for an indefinite period, perhaps for life, the slave of the creditor. It is a common thing to hear the wife of a working man exclaim, "O, I wish often that people would not trust me so much!" But then this is when payment is called for, and she is in a fair way of having her wish gratified.

One word in behalf of those who are struggling with debts, and have hard work to keep their heads above water. There are many such. They are in the mire, and the difficulty is how to get out. Not naturally dishonest, they are so much the more sensitive; and dread walking up street or being seen in any public place for fear of encountering that ugly apparition, their impatient creditor. How ardently they wish that at the outset of housekeeping life they had attended more to the maxims of economy, and lived within their means. But alas! it is now too late. Their goods are tottering around their hearths, and in all likelihood before long will be seized by the ruthless broker, and their homes become desolate! Above everything they hate the stinging reflection that they are not as good as their word—that the confidence reposed in them is destroyed. The harrassing, festering, torturing thought, which burdens their spirits day and night, is how to recover themselves; but their way appears hedged up, and, sinking under the pressure of circumstances, they are ready to despair. The effort required to sustain one's self in such a position is almost heroic. How great then the moral energy requisite for emancipation! Nevertheless, with a determined will—the whole family working together for this end—much may be done. Let it be seen that self-sacrifices can be made, that retrenchment in the mode of living is practised, that strong drink as a beverage is given up, and the strictest frugality persevered in, and things will soon begin to mend, and probably sympathetic assistance be obtained. Let the benevolent see that self-help is vigorously at work, and it is almost certain that they will not allow the really struggling family to fall into abject beggary and disgrace. Some kind friend will, perhaps, be found who will undertake to advance the sum required to free them, in the shape of a loan to be repaid by small instalments. In many cases this would be better than a gift; for although, as we have said, it is impossible to borrow one's self out of debt, yet the pressure would be removed without expense, and the energy required would be likely to be kept up and continued. I am inclined to think that much good might be done by the wealthy in this way, by a sum set apart for the purpose. Were good faith observed by the borrower—and if the reformation be real this would be the case—the sum might be worked over and over again without the receiver being degraded by taking a benefaction; whereas, if it were bestowed as a gift, it could only be applied once, and that with but dubious results. The rich have in this way a leverage at command which, if used, might be the means of lifting from the hearts and homes of the desolate, a crushing load of sorrow and distress.

I have lingered thus long upon the subject of debt, because I think it of great importance in social economy. Debt is the cause of more misunderstanding and injustice than anything else. The amount of bad debts incurred by the working class, especially in small towns, where people are more familiar with each other than in large ones, is incalculable, and it should be remembered that the burden of these debts falls upon the consumer. The retail trader generally reckons a per centage for losses, and fixes the price of his commodity accordingly, so that the honest customer is taxed to make good the defalcations of his less scrupulous, improvident, or unfortunate neighbour.

Again: *Be cautious as to visiting, and entertaining company.* I have known more than one family wrecked from this cause alone. At their wedding it may be they have invited a score or two of friends, and this has cost as much as would have maintained them for a month. Then there are visits and return visits, for which preparations must be made, and fare of a better than ordinary kind provided. This practice is not only costly, but it is a great tax upon the time of a working-man (and time to him is money), as well as inclining his mind towards dissipation. It is all very well to be social, and to have a friend with whom to enjoy a leisure hour and a frugal meal; but to have too many associates and acquaintances is an evil, expensive and pernicious. Akin to this is also the too prevalent custom of indulging in cheap railway trips, and the celebration of holidays and festivals. This is the growing fault of the age, and is quite opposed to maxims of prudence and economy. A railway trip to enjoy the beauties of nature, or a visit to a large town, is excellent as a treat, after a workman has been pent up for months in a confined position; but such pleasures should be sparingly indulged in, and care should be taken that they do not trench too much upon the income, and also that they are not undertaken from a love of mere gossip rather than of calm, rational enjoyment. It is very galling to a tradesman to see a person who is in his debt flaunting along the street in gay attire, in haste to catch a holiday train, to disburse the hard-earned money among strangers when it should have found its way into his till. The middle classes in small towns situate near railways, have severely felt the evils of these trips, as well as the poor themselves. The undue observance of holiday seasons has also seriously embarrassed many a working man. What with the time consumed and the feast provided, the cost is such, that one is scarcely got over before another arrives, and the mind is therefore in a continual worry and pester. Many of these observances are continued more from custom than from any intrinsic gratification gained by them. I have often heard people say at the close of holidays, they were glad they were over; but the tyrant Custom is so powerful that the next season has found them feasting as gaily as ever. In reference to holiday-making, as well as other pleasures, an economist will always put the question to himself, "Can I afford them?" And he will take into consideration not merely the time and money expended, but how far they unhinge the mind and unfit him for the regular business of life. It always takes more or less time to settle down to work after a holiday.

Another maxim should be *cleanliness and neatness.* I have already hinted at the important bearing of these qualities on Household Economy. It may be easily shown, and has been proved over and over again by sanatory statistics, that cleanliness both of the person and of the house is essential to health, and we all know that sickness is expensive. Clothes and furniture also by being kept clean are made the best of and rendered more durable. Dirt is apt to rot linen and clothing generally, and sometimes on this account they will drop into tatters whilst in wear. Furniture is worth far more if kept bright, and will last longer than if allowed to corrode by damp, filth, and negligence. The love of neatness is invaluable in a wife, on the score of saving alone. It will turn every bit of ribbon and half-worn garment to the best account, and contrive to make a comfortable and even charming appearance with things which others would put into the rag-basket as refuse. It is this quality of neatness which often constitutes the real secret of *thrift ;* for the person possessing it is forbid by a natural taste, and love of severe and modest beauty, to indulge in vulgar pride and extravagance. On the contrary, these expensive vices are viewed with feelings of dislike and disgust.

The art of cooking and preparing food ought not to be passed over in treating of Household Economy. It is but little studied by the wives and daughters of the labouring classes, but attention to it would be very beneficial. There is often a great deal of waste caused by sheer ignorance of the art of preparing a meal. The virtue of the food is lost in the pot or the oven through the imperfect process, or the dish is served up in an insipid state, when a few herbs properly mixed with it would have rendered it palatable and savoury. In cooking animal food, care should be taken to obtain from it the whole of the nourishing juices it is capable of yielding, and even the bones and offal should be turned to account; they will be found useful for broths and soups, or glutinous jellies. In making a pudding, or bread, care is required in the kneading which is often a delicate and difficult operation; but it depends upon the skill with which it is performed, whether the paste or the bread be a heavy indigestible mass, or light, agreeable, and wholesome. The plentiful supply of fish in the inland districts, since the opening of railways, is a great boon to the working classes. It is now brought to almost every door in a good and wholesome state, at a very low price, and often affords a cheap and satisfying meal, but from some cause or other it is not taken to by the working classes so much as might have been supposed. Perhaps the rough and unskilful manner of preparing it for table may be one cause of its being neglected. I would close my few remarks on this head by recommending as a household book Mrs. Rundell's Domestic Cookery, which may be bought for a shilling,* and teaches the whole art professedly on the most economical principles. It should be studied by every housewife.

Another thing of prime importance in Economy is *the diligent use of the needle.* This little bit of glittering

---

* Routledge and Co., Publishers, Farringdon-street, London.

steel is almost as serviceable to the cottager as to the mariner. By its constant and skilful use the industrious housewife

"Can make auld clothes seem maist as weel's the new,"

and can so manage that the garments which the senior members of the family have outgrown or cast aside shall appear to advantage on the juniors successively. I have often admired the clever way in which clothes are remodelled by an industrious and handy housewife. Tom having outgrown his jacket and trousers, they are turned and re-cut, and garnished with a new row of buttons, and little Bob is as proud of them, and struts about in them with as jaunty an air as though they were a bran new suit from the tailor's shop. Bobby, renovated, looks smart in them for years, and all the while a wee bit brother is longing for the happy day when they will descend to him, and he will toddle in them to church or chapel. Such contrivances are an immense saving to a man with a family, as is also the making up, darning, and the repairing of the garments the family require. A woman handy with her needle is, in short, a valuable help-mate to a working man; and the possessor of such a partner cannot prize her too highly, as upon her exertions he is in a great measure dependent for his domestic comfort and prosperity.

I will only allude at length to one more important consideration in the practice of Household Economy, viz., *Making provision for a time of need.* No economy can be complete without this, for a time of adversity will come as surely as night follows the day. It is now customary for working men who wish to preserve their respectability, to join a Sick Benefit Society. This is laudable, but care should be taken to join those which are formed on the best principles, and are under the safeguard of the law. Even in these there is a difference; some are managed far better than others, and some meet at a public-house, where a part of the savings are spent in drink. Indeed, some of these ought rather to be called Eating and Drinking Societies than Sick Clubs. There is in these days plenty of choice as to the club the respectable working man can enter, and it becomes him to use judgement and precaution. Let him be sure that it is founded upon safe principles; that its capital is properly invested; that its rules are fair and upright; and that it is legally enrolled. It becomes a family when practicable, to enter into a club to ensure medical attendance and medicine; for doctor's bills are often very high, and their discharge is a serious burden to a working man. But sickness is not the only contingency which may beset a family. There are, every now and then, paroxysms in commerce, when employment ceases, or becomes scarce and precarious. Such seasons will be anticipated by every wise man and woman, and endeavours will be made to meet them. And then there is the time of old age, which often creeps on almost imperceptibly, when the strong man is bowed down, and the eyes become dim and the ear deaf. It is the paramount duty of all who can, to lay up against this season, and the sooner it is begun the better. On these accounts, savings' banks and penny banks are established; the latter, especially, are admirable institutions, as they beget a habit in children and young people of saving their little perquisites and gains, and show them the importance of attending to little things.

One boy spends his pence in cakes or marbles, and becomes a thoughtless, improvident man; another takes them weekly to the secretary of a penny bank, and by the time he is out of his teens, he is the possessor of a little hoard which may give him the start in life as well as the bias of a saving disposition. And then, again, for those who have the command of somewhat larger sums of money, there are the life insurances, which, for a small annual premium, secure to the policy-holder an annuity when in the decline of life, or a payment, in case of death, sufficient to allow the bereaved family still to hold up their heads. Young men, the money which many of you spend on tobacco alone, might purchase you one of these policies, and secure to you the sweet reflection that you have made provision against the dark and cloudy day!

It will be seen from the above observations, how prominent a part a *wife* bears in the practice of Household Economy. Hence the importance of imparting a sound and practical knowledge of housekeeping to all young females. In this respect, many daughters of working men are sadly deficient. Sent at a very early age to the mill or the factory, and kept there during the whole of their maiden state, and some of them long after wedlock, they are totally unfit for housewives, being quite ignorant of household work. It is lamentable to see the slatternly way in which some young wives engage in cooking and cleaning, whilst as to sewing, a needle is seldom seen between their fingers. Things, therefore, soon go wrong, and when the good man comes home from work, there is no clean-swept hearth, snug seat, or cheery little fairy wife to welcome him. His food is spoiled in the cooking, or half cold, and he is chilled or angry with the aspect of the room, and the slovenly appearance of his partner. Thus by degrees he neglects his home, which, alas, is no home to him, and wanders into scenes of dissipation to kill time, or to afford him some amusement in lieu of domestic comfort. Many a poor, well-meaning, hard-working man, is placed in these circumstances, and now bitterly regrets entering into the marriage state without seeking a more thrifty partner. Economy requires a perfect understanding between man and wife, and a hearty co-operation in the wise management of household affairs.

The important bearing of a comfortable and commodious dwelling must not be overlooked. It is often the miserable dwelling that induces slovenly and dirty habits, and then follow fevers and pestilential diseases. Better to give an extra sixpence or shilling rent per week than to settle down in one of those miserable huts which some griping landlords build for their poor tenantry, regardless of their comfort, and thinking of nothing but the per-centage the tenements will yield. Without doubt, if in country places, convenient cottages were more frequently built for the peasantry, with plots of ground attached, to furnish vegetables for the family use, the cottager would be more in love with his home, and the moral and physical condition of the poor would be improved. I am glad to see that public attention has been directed to this subject; if generally carried out, a great social reformation will be sure to follow. In some villages known to the writer it has been done, and the families are so different to what they were twenty years back, that they do not seem to be the same race.

Before closing this subject, I would just hold out a caution against confounding household economy with parsimony, meanness, and covetousness. I have heard it objected to on this account; and, without doubt, this, as well as most other good things, is liable to abuse. An economical person may degenerate into a miser, but this does not follow as a natural consequence, and it is only when its maxims are carried out, that, with the working classes, there is much opportunity of being open-handed and generous. It is a spurious liberality which makes free with the goods of another; but the practice of economy with respect to our worldly goods would leave a margin for the cultivation of benevolence. Let all then, rich and poor, join heart and hand in endeavouring to cherish and diffuse the prudential maxims of economy, which would tend largely to promote unity and happiness amongst us. There would then be little straining after effect, little aping of the class just above the aspirant, which leads to so much folly and misery; but, happy in the calm delights of a quiet home, the peasantry and artisans of England would realise the beautiful picture presented in Cotton's "Fireside,"—a short poem which I would recommend for perusal as worth all the ranting heroics ever penned. Happy in the bosom of his family, and with a mind at ease, the working man would then in his own ingle nook, cultivate the study of letters, and, banishing "malice, envy, and all uncharitableness," would probably aspire after the "peace that passeth all understanding" by the culture and practice of piety.

Prose Fictions:
THEIR USES AND ABUSES.

EVERY one who is at all acquainted with the literature of the present century, must be aware that it is characterised by a very large number of Prose Fictions. The relative merit and numerical proportion of this description of authorship far exceed that of any former period. The graphic pens which have been employed in this department of literature, have delineated character and manners the most varied, described scenes the most opposite, and have given us vivid pictures of man and woman, as they are found in the most different situations possible—amid the grandeur and etiquette of courts and palaces—the conventionalism of middle life—and, not the least interesting, amusing, or instructive, as they exist in the humblest, the rudest, and the most primitive or degraded condition. And not only are the spirit and manners of the present age thus strikingly pourtrayed, but the events of by-gone periods have furnished ample themes for the writers of romance and fiction. The chivalry of the middle ages especially is gilded by their glowing pencils, softening its sterner features, and flinging around it a radiance like that of the setting sun over the distant hills or the hoary castle, thereby transforming what would otherwise be gloomy and forbidding, into a picture radiant with glory or softened with mellow lustre. A deep insight into the philosophy of human nature also characterises these writers. The heart is laid bare by them, and its most secret cogitations and springs of action revealed, which, "as face answereth to face in water," correspond to the feelings and sentiments of the reader. The world of fancy and imagination is also peculiarly the province in which they revel at will, calling forth the wildest and most grotesque objects as easily as the possessor of the wonderful lamp is said to have summoned his attendant Genii or Prospero to make use of his wand of enchantment.

The great writers of Prose Fiction have gained for themselves a high niche in the temple of Fame, while the very nature of their works insures them a popularity far exceeding that of other authors. The writings of Defoe, Fielding, Scott, Bulwer Lytton, Marriott, Cooper, Dickens, and other novelists, are in demand by the reading public far beyond scientific, metaphysical, historical, or theological works, or perhaps those of any other kind; while the immortal allegory of Bunyan, the artless yet fascinating tale of Oliver Goldsmith, and the recent remarkable book of Mrs. Stowe, have had a world-wide fame and have become "familiar as household words."* Were this department of literature

---

* The following facts, which form the substance of a paragraph in a number of the *Athenæum*, indicate the comparative popularity of authors in the manufacturing capital. They are con-

confined to authors of the class I have mentioned, there would probably be but little danger of evil accruing from their perusal. They are not perhaps more characterized by their extraordinary merit than by their healthy tone. Indeed it is a fact which the history of

---

tained in the report of the Manchester Free Library, and I have thought it might not be uninteresting to transcribe them here:—

"Shakespere is the writer most in demand; his works, and books illustrating these works having been issued 352 successive times within the first year. The book next in popularity to Shakespere is 'The Arabian Nights,' which in the year found 294 readers. Scott and Defoe come next in rank. 'Ivanhoe' was issued 241 times, 'Robinson Crusoe' 239 times. The latter author seems to be a great favourite, all his principal stories being in great demand: 'Moll Flanders' was issued 237 times; 'Roxana,' 108; 'Colonel Jacque,' 170; 'Captain Singleton,' 170. Swift's "Gulliver' was read 123 times; Smollett's 'Roderick Random," 82. Biography has been much read. In the history of England, Macaulay is the popular favorite. His history has been read by 124; the Pictorial, by 60; Lingard, by 41; Hume, by 31 persons. French history, especially of the Napoleonic time, has been in great demand. Many of the books appear to have been glanced at and laid aside. Two readers appear to have gone through Hume; fourteen attacked Clarendon, but only three reached the seventh volume; the same number toiled through Lingard. Of the crowd who began with Allison, only one reached the close of the history. Books of travel, shipwreck, and adventure, have been asked for very often. Mr. Cumming almost divided the honours with Defoe. Dana's 'Two years before the Mast' has had 74 readers, and Mr. Layard's 'Nineveh' the same number."

I think these statistics afford some useful information, and were they given from public libraries generally, they would furnish no bad index to the mental tastes and cultivation of the people. As an example of the enormous sale of "Uncle Tom's Cabin," I may mention a statement that has gone the round of the newspapers,—that a publishing house in London has cleared by that book alone, £15,000.

literature will bear out, that morality and virtue go hand in hand with the highest genius and ability; and it may be predicated as a certainty, that if a writer pander to vice, inculcate principles of doubtful morality, or lend himself as the vehicle of sensuality and sin, he will never reach the acme of renown; or, having attained it, he will surely fall from his high eminence, and degenerate into the mere scribbler—a fool among wise men, though regarded as a wise man among fools. Still, it is a lamentable truth, that in our own day a large class of authors have sprung up, whose writings find their way into the workshop or on to the cottage shelf, in the form of cheap publications, and work incalculable mischief. These are eagerly devoured by those (and, alas! their number is legion), whose gross tastes and limited intelligence will not allow them to relish or appreciate the better class of fictions. They afford poisons which are sweet to the morbid and depraved mental appetite, but whose tendency is only to increase that morbidity and deepen that depravity. I have often mourned over the rush that is made to the shop of the retailer of misnomered cheap publications of this trashy kind, while better works remain uncalled for and unbought. But the fact furnishes a true index to the state of popular morals and mental culture, and is rather a consequence than a cause of the unsatisfactory state of the education of the million. Whenever a decided improvement takes place in the mental condition of the masses (and there are signs of its rapid approach), the morbid productions of such writers as G. W. M. Reynolds, Ainsworth, and Eugene Sue, will give place to others of a more healthy and intellectual kind. Until then, the only directions I can give for their use are similar to the advice of the late Dr. Abernethy, respecting the proper way of dressing a cucumber—that it should be cut into slices, peppered and salted, and then thrown away. So, I would say, the best way of using these books is to take them to the huxters or the trunkmakers, and get them used up.

But as the more healthy and legitimate kind of Prose Fictions forms the staple of light literature, and as their market is daily widening and increasing, some remarks as to their uses and abuses may not be altogether unprofitable, especially as they now find their way very largely into the public libraries of the nation. Concerning the manner in which they are to be used by the reader, it is impossible to lay down any fixed rules. The diversity of mental tastes and of intellectual pursuits would continually interfere with giving any stated quantum of this kind of reading, or with the exact manner of perusing it. In these respects the judicious reader will be a law unto himself, which must differ according to circumstances. My observations in relation to this part of the subject must therefore be of the most general kind, and are rather meant for the tyro, whose mental character and habits are not yet formed, than for persons of more advanced life. To such I would respectfully tender the following advice:—

Firstly.—Do not abuse works of Fiction by reading them to the neglect of more substantial studies. There is great danger of this owing to their fascination. The imagination is the most absorbing as well as the livliest of our mental faculties, and the diversion afforded by it is shewn in very early life. Every child is enchanted by tales and fictitious stories, the more wonderful the better. And the surprising adventures, the thrilling catastrophes, and the novel passion of love, which form so large an ingredient in most novels and romances, all unite in withdrawing the attention of youth from more laborious yet necessary studies. Happily these severer pursuits are not destitute of the romantic ingredient which makes fictitious narratives so engaging. Truth is said to be strange—stranger than fiction—a proverb, the force of which every one who knows anything of science or historical events must admit. The most ingeniously-wrought tale appears clumsily constructed when compared with some of the actual occurrences of history; and incidents are to be found in the experience of most persons, which in a novel would be thought highly improbable. And when the attention of the student is turned to the sublime truths of chemistry, geology, or astronomy, he will find that his fancy cannot grasp the wonderful facts which they elicit. Think of the startling discoveries which science has revealed in our own day. Can the "Arabian Nights" vie with the wonders she has called forth? Are the genii of fancy swifter than the electric telegraph, or more potent than the steam engine? Does the wonderful lamp of eastern fiction equal the lamp of science? Or do the wildest writers of romance dare to sketch in fancy anything comparable to her realizations? The youth whose attention is turned in this direction need not let his faculty of wonder lie dormant; but will find in his scientific studies, ample room for his imagination. But if he neglect these elementary and severer pursuits; nay if he do not gain an intimate acquaintance with them (especially with history, geography, and the classics), he cannot enter into the spirit, or fully enjoy the beauties, of fictitious literature. No authors perhaps take so much for granted, or suppose a person to be so thoroughly conversant with knowledge of every kind, as the great masters of Prose Fiction. Without a knowledge of British History, and of the feudalism and chivalry of Europe in the middle ages, it is impossible to appreciate the tales of the author of "Waverly;" and one of the most interesting fictions of Bulwer Lytton is founded upon the excavations of Pompeii, and the manners of the Greeks and Neapolitans of the first century. These works are therefore infinitely more entertaining to any one previously acquainted with classic manners and the Pompeian discoveries, than to those ignorant of them. Indeed this may be one chief cause why these and similar great authors are not more popular. The uninformed reader cannot appreciate their beauties or meaning, because he does not understand them; and he therefore prefers the more common-place, and to him more intelligible writers. It is consequently essential to youth to lay a solid foundation of learning, in order fully to relish the best writers of fiction at all. Their works are the ornament of literature, constituting its "Corinthian capital," beautiful on the summit, but which, without the solid shaft and firm base, would be but unsubstantial and unseemly figments. Those who confine themselves in the morning of their days to a promiscuous reading of novels and romances, to the neglect of the severer studies, will necessarily become at best but superficial thinkers; while for the want of general knowledge, they will be incapable of fully realising or reading aright the chief authors in the department they have chosen.

Secondly.—Do not abuse these works by reading them hastily and superficially, but *study* them, especially as regards the *character* delineated and the *philosophy* imparted. It is a mistaken notion to suppose that a work of fiction which is worth reading, can be hurriedly perused with benefit, or even with pleasure of a high kind. But I think this error is very general. "O," says one, "it is only a novel. I can soon skim through it; it does not require much thought." Perhaps not, but if so, throw it on one side, for it is not worth your attention at all. And the character of a book in this respect may be generally known before a half-dozen pages are gone through. Time is too short and far too precious to be wasted upon such frivolities, especially when books of a better class are constantly presented and are so easy of access. But the fault does not always lie with the volume. The reader does not peruse it philosophically. He hurries after the incidents as a hunter after game—helter-skelter, in a break-neck course through (or rather over) chapter after chapter, that he may arrive at the catastrophe and be in at the death. And as the sportsman, eager after his game, heeds not the beautiful scenery around him, and cannot stay to notice the modest flowers that bloom in his path; so such a reader, almost entirely regardless of the beauty, elegance, and power of description, or of the pithy sentences which in some fictions so felicitously abound, hastes forward to know how matters will turn out in the developement of the tale. But books of this character ought not to be read for incident alone. The delineation of character, and the other beauties to which I have referred, oftentimes constitute their chief merit. The characters drawn by Sir Walter Scott, in particular, are well worthy the attention of everyone, and are not to be scanned over in haste, but should be looked at again and again. For it is with his works as with almost everything of the highest order. The mind cannot take them in at the first glance. They seem to grow and expand at every repeated perusal, and will well repay a most earnest study. There are often also in his tales, especially in "Waverley," charming little sentences of a proverbial character, full of pithy morality, and others of the deepest pathos, or of the keenest satire, each of which sparkle like gems on almost every page. I would also here refer to those two charming little works of Longfellow, " Hyperion " and " Kavanagh," which abound with the most felicitous expressions and the richest description; whose incidents are of the commonest kind, and are evidently merely pegs whereon to hang the observations of the author. Both these works will repay the most devoted attention of the reader. But however the catastrophe of a tale may turn out, or whether its incidents be more or less surprising or diverting, the tale will surely be no less relished, by gaining an intimate acquaintance with its details, and a thorough insight into its characters and its philosophy. On the contrary, such a knowledge will greatly tend to heighten its interest.

Thirdly.—Do not read works of fiction to the neglect of the more serious duties of life, but let them be perused at proper seasons. Youth need especial caution in this respect, as perhaps these works are a greater evil in causing a neglect of duty than in any other way. On account of their exciting and amusing qualities, they are often indulged in so freely, that such indulgence becomes a habit; and as the appetite grows by what it feeds upon, every spare minute (and many a minute which can ill be spared), is devoted to this insatiate propensity, until a vice is formed of the most pernicious kind, and leading to the worst consequences. Of these I shall speak hereafter. "Moderation," or else "total abstinence," as regards indulgence in fiction, is the duty of every one, or the soul will get intoxicated by the absorbing passion, to the ruin of the mental and moral character. Beware, youthful reader especially, of these seductions! Because the gratification of this passion can be indulged in without its attracting much attention from others, and can be pursued without the expense attached to more active pleasures, greater watchfulness is required, and more diligence should be observed. Where a propensity to this abuse exists in an individual, I would recommend him to ballast his mind by a system of more solid reading and study, as having not only a tendency to strengthen it, but to wean his attention from such deleterious pursuits, and counteract and neutralise their pernicious influence. Like most other pleasures, the gratification of this taste may be good in moderation, and is especially adapted for hours of leisure and relaxation. To seasons of indisposition, works of imagination are peculiarly suited, and will frequently cure the mind of *ennui* better than anything else. To be read to advantage too, they should be adapted to the particular time and place of their perusal—a kind of sympathy should exist between the surroundings of the reader and the subject of his volume. Thus, how is the dramatic effect of the "Bride of Lammermoor" heightened by being read in a solitary spot, upon a winter night, when the wind is moaning in fitful gusts, as it did around the desolate castle of Wolf's Crag. "The Monastery" and "The Abbott" are also winter tales; whilst I should prefer reading "Waverley" in the pleasant summer-time, seated on the new-mown hay, or in an arbour of jessamines or honeysuckles. An ancient ruin or venerable edifice is also adapted to many tales of romance, as is also a wood or forest. Each of the seasons has also its particular tales. Especially is Christmas appropriate to many. Indeed this ancient festival has long been renowned for story-telling; and owing to the associations with which it is entwined, the friends that it musters round the hearth, and the reflections it calls forth, this is naturally accounted for. The weird tales that are then often recited or read, possess a magic charm, and form no inconsiderable part of the luxury of the season. Should the student therefore wish to enjoy nature and the recurring seasons to the greatest advantage, let him take an appropriate prose fiction and muse over its pages, while everything about him is in harmony with, and suggestive of the subject upon which he dwells.

Having given these few directions as to the manner of reading fictions in general, I would briefly refer to the advantages to be derived from their perusal.

The antiquity of parables, fables, and fictitious narratives and the prominent place which they have ever held in the literature of all nations, sufficiently denote them to be one of the most striking, natural, and potent methods of instruction to be found. Some indeed have objected to the use of fables or children, on the ground of the danger of their taking for literal truth the stories which they read. This objection I think of very little weight. It proceeds from estimating too lowly the apprehension of children, which is generally more acute than we give them credit for. I have never yet found the boy or girl who could read, taking for truth the tale of a lion or a fox holding a discourse. I think with the poet Cowper, that

> —" the boy who knows no better
> Than to interpret by the letter,
>   A story of a cock or bull,
> Must have a most uncommon skull."

But should such a blockhead here and there be found, his after experience must soon correct his mistake, and a very few years will suffice for him to out-grow his duncehood, if he ever out-grow it at all.

But objections such as these generally arise from the desire of individuals to appear singular, rather than from any other motive. I would therefore dismiss such fastidious reformers, by asking them to furnish proofs of any evil which has ever resulted from this amusing mode of imparting knowledge, and proceed briefly to notice the larger number who object to fictitious reading generally, on the ground of its being adverse to religion and morality.

The severe and puritanical tastes of many of our forefathers, and some of our contemporaries, have led them to forbid and to condemn the whole mass of novels and romances, as being injurious to public and private morals, and of a decidedly irreligious tendency. And indeed the character of many of this kind of writings justifies such condemnation. The dramas and romances of the last two centuries often made vice alluring, and abetted profligacy and folly. By these means the rake was regarded as a fashionable gentleman, and the man of real virtue was held up to ridicule. So much was this the case, that it required the powerful pens of Addison, Steele, Johnson, and their coadjutors, to correct the evil, reform society, and repair the injuries entailed. I would not for a moment countenance the perusal of such works. They are fast floating down the stream of time towards Lethe's wharf. There let them perish, and give place to others of a more wholesome and virtuous kind. But let not prose fictions be indiscriminately condemned because of these pernicious productions. The question is, Is this kind of literature necessarily injurious? Is there anything in it intrisically bad, or that leads to bad results? I might reply by calling attention to the fact that the Great Teacher himself employed parabolic and fictitious narratives very largely in His discourses, and thereby set His seal of approbation upon such methods of conveying and illustrating truth. And so long as human nature is what it is, the amusing will be tolerated by society at large, notwithstanding the frowns of the over-righteous, and the condemnations of the austere, who labour in vain to bring others to their own strait-laced opinions, and have no charity for those that differ.—"Thinkest thou that because thou art virtuous there shall be no more cakes and ale? Yes, by Saint Anne, and ginger shall be hot in the mouth too!"*

The large class of fictitious writings called "historical," I would especially recommend to the youthful reader, as affording a powerful auxiliary to the study of history. Every one who carefully reads them, must thereby gain an acquaintance with the events upon which they treat; and these events are generally more brilliantly and richly coloured than in the sober pages of veritable history; and oftentimes more light is thrown upon the habits and customs of mankind by them than by the dry records of legitimate chroniclers. The tales of Sir Walter Scott are in this respect of immense value; not only for the information they afford, which is very great; but also because they beget a love of historical research, the reader being naturally anxious to obtain all the information he can connected with what has so deeply interested him. And as the best novelists owe much of their celebrity to the associations connected with the places which they have embellished, so they have in their turn imparted fresh attractions to these spots, and rendered the events they have chosen to illustrate, more intensely interesting and engaging. One, therefore, helps and beautifies the other; the informed and educated reader gaining the advantages of both, and gathering thereby a vintage of the richest and most lusciuus intellectual fruit.

Again, the writers of fiction have rendered the world a great service by their graphic delineation of character and manners. This has been done very happily by some of our late novelists. There is scarcely any peculiarity by which one person is distinguished from

---

* Shakspeare.

another, which has not been graphically pourtrayed by their pens. The study therefore of their works shows us human nature as it exists in all its various phases, and we thereby gain an intimate acquaintance with it—a kind of philosophy which, next to self-knowledge, is perhaps the most useful to be found. By the study of these works the mind is enlarged and refined, the manners polished, and the mental taste improved; for next to mingling with the best classes of society, the intimacy we gain by being acquainted with them through the medium of books is most to be prized. I believe the gross tastes and vulgar amusements of many of the uneducated to be mainly owing to their ignorance. Could they but be brought to relish the best writers of fiction, they would soon disregard the coarse gratifications of which they are now so fond, and which are commonly so expensive. The race-course, the betting table, the ale bench, and the theatre, would be abandoned, as affording less amusement and excitement even, than can be gained from the shelves of a library, and at a cost trifling in comparison. I am of opinion that even the trashy kind of reading to which allusion has before been made, has not been without its value in this respect, inasmuch as it is a step in advance of the old boorish and brutal amusements. I think, too, that a careful perusal of the works of Sir Walter Scott and Bulwer Lytton is far more likely to make a finished gentleman than a study of Chesterfield. The characters of their heroes and heroines, are more adapted to stamp their impress upon the mind, and captivate the heart, than the maxims and rules of the polite philosopher. Such tales also impart a taste for the sublime and beautiful, the grotesque and wild; bring the mind into unison with the many-sounding chords of nature, and cause the heart to respond to her in her various moods; while the supernatural and spiritual machinery employed, draws the soul into contact with the infinite, and excites and gratifies the imagination.

Further, the moral inductions of the best fictions are of the most salutary nature. To refer again to the works of our great novelist, the lessons he teaches in them are highly beneficial. Look for instance at the filial love and sisterly affection of Jeanie Deans, and at her heroism and virtue. If a young woman can rise from the perusal of the story of her conflicts and achievements in her sister's behalf without being benefitted, she is either the best or the worst of her sex. Then again, what a warning is afforded in the "Bride of Lammermoor" against parental interference with the marriage of their children for their own selfish purposes! How strikingly are the evils of political fanaticism shown in "Waverley," and religious fanaticism, enthusiasm, and persecution, in "Old Mortality!" In short, there is not a tale that Scott has written but bears a moral which appeals to the heart and fixes itself there. I think the study of such works as these, constitutes a better moral training (when read aright), than can be gained by a whole system of ethics. They are more impressive; and, calling forth largely the sympathetic influences, they stimulate the soul to virtuous thought and action.

The only other use of Prose Fictions to which I shall refer, is their supplying an excellent fund of amusement for hours of solitude and indisposition. Is a person, through stress of weather, detained at a country inn or lone house, ready to be devoured of *ennui,* because he cannot engage in the active pleasures or business of life? Does he seek for relief in watching the drops of rain coursing down the window, or the dripping poultry or cattle, which are the only objects that meet his view from without? Is he with a sigh ready to count himself as among the most miserable of his species? A work of fiction, accidentally taken up, beguiles the weary time, until he confesses that the minutes fly too fast, and the day which promised to be so cheerless, is looked back upon as one of the red-letter days of his life.

These works too are eminently adapted for the invalid, when both body and mind are enfeebled by indisposition, and the patient cannot take a part in anything requiring severe thought. Then it is that the lagging hours are relieved of their tedium as if by enchantment, and the powerful imagination of the author

—" Takes the troubled soul,
And laps it in Elysium."

Every one who has at all entered into the spirit of these works, must hail them as an invaluable boon for such seasons. And it is perhaps not too much to say that the writings of the author of " Waverly " have done as much good, simply as curatives, as the medical prescriptions of all his contemporary physicians. How delightful is it to have these sources of amusement open to us when we are unfit to engage in anything else! How cheap, and easy of access are they! A book under one's pillow at such a season, is a luxury which prince and peasant can enjoy, and with equal zest, provided the mind be sufficiently informed to appreciate it. This is one of the most general and most advantageous uses of Prose Fictions.

A word or two on the evil consequences of their abuse. One of these is the tendency to enervate the intellect. Such writings act upon the mind as narcotics and anodynes do upon the nervous system, stimulating it at first, but if indulged in too freely, prostrating and paralysing it. In this process the mind becomes intoxicated, and sees everything through a false medium. The man led captive by his imagination, becomes quite unfit for the stern realities of life, and its sober duties are neglected, or become burdensome in the extreme. The slave of this habit, indeed, passes his days in a feverish dream, the sweet and simple charms of nature losing their interest, until the trials and difficulties which beset him awaken him from his delirious vision, and he finds himself unmanned and unequal to encounter them. What opium is to Orientals, novels and romances are to Europeans; the consequences of them being similarly disastrous. Another evil of this abuse is that it generates selfishness in the heart, deadens sensibility, and renders the individual callous to the woes and sufferings of others. Many a one will weep over a tale of fictitious sorrow or wrong, who has no sympathy with real distress. Such sentimental and theatrical feeling is but a form of intense selfishness; it rarely accompanies genuine philanthrophy, but rather resembles the state of mind of those tyrants, who put their victims to death, for the pleasure of witnessing their dying throes. Too much familiarity with this unreal woe, also renders the heart less alive to cases of real sorrow, just because the mind is used to contemplate it. Every one knows that the heart soon becomes deadened by use and habit towards what at first greatly impressed and affected it.

The last evil consequence of this abuse to which I shall allude, is its tendency to confuse, disturb, and distort veritable history, and fact, and confound them with fable and fiction. This is often a vice of the writer as well as of the reader. The result has been the entanglement of truth and history in the web of fable, giving rise to the multitude of false legends which have assumed the garb of real events, and, passing for facts, have deceived so many in every age. A novelist ought to be extremely careful how he embellishes the page of history, and on no account should he allow himself to distort and corrupt it. And the reader should be as careful not to let the incidents of fiction mix in his mind with sober fact, if he wish to preserve a true and faithful remembrance of the details of history.

Before closing the subject, I would impress upon the youthful reader (for whom these observations are especially intended), the importance of care in the selection of his books; and would advise him to be sparing in the use of fictitious literature, and to see that it is of sterling quality. The issue of cheap editions of first-rate works, is a boon which places them within his reach, and it is his own fault if he prefer inferior productions. The proper and moderate use of these great authors he will find a valuable help to the acquisition of knowledge, as well as a source of delightful entertainment. But if he abuse them, by preferring them to the study of truth, he will at best find himself in a "fool's paradise," among the most superficial and vain of mankind. And when he awakes from his delusive dream (as awake he must), he will find his intellect enervated, his mind uninformed, his time misspent, and himself a frivolous idle *fiction* in a world of serious realities.

Psyche:

THE IMMATERIALITY OF THE MIND,

AND THE

IMMORTALITY OF THE SOUL.

THE nature and destiny of the mind or soul of man, comprehending those sublime faculties which distinguish the human from all other sentient creatures of which we are cognizant, is surely a subject of the first importance, and of the most intense interest. No sooner does Reason expand her powers, and Imagination plume her wings—no sooner does Mind develope its nature, and begin to *think*, than the thinker finds himself substantially related to those mighty intelligences who have subdued the stubborn elements to their will; who have scaled the summits of the earth, explored its depths, navigated its seas, analyzed its matter, defined its figure, motions and size, tamed and brought into servitude its inferior animals; and who, in short, by the force of mental power exerted over inert and organized nature, have won for themselves, beyond dispute, the glorious title of "lords of the creation."

And if he turn from the triumphs of his race over

what is merely *physical*,* to consider its nobler and more ideal achievements, man finds still more admirable proofs of his sublime capacities. The glowing canvass, the graceful statue, the marvellous edifice, the graphic history, the subtle disquisition, the immortal poem;— all these are so many trophies, which attest the dignity of his species; and, swelling his soul with noble aspirations, invite him to lofty emulation. And although there are comparatively few who possess this semi-creative or delineative faculty, which is termed *genius*; and whilst the number who can appreciate these intellectual works, though much greater, is small indeed, even in civilized nations; yet where is there an individual who at all exercies his mental faculties, that is not at one time or other, startled at his own powers?— whose imagination does not launch out into the infinite; whose thoughts do not strive to lay hold on the eternal; whose emotions are not too big for utterance, who does not feel himself to be indeed fearfully and wonderfully endowed? And yet how humiliating is the fact that the whole human family, in common with the meanest thing that breathes, must bow to a mysterious and inevitable law, that interferes with all their designs, and terminates all their operations! By disease and death, man's fairest hopes are frustrated, his grandest attempts renederd abortive, and his dearest wishes disappointed.

---

* The author has used the word "physical" in the sense of "corporeal" throughout the Essay. But while using it, he thought perhaps he was not employing it with strict correctness as there is the physics of the mind. The word is derived from the Greek word φυσιχος, (phusixos)—natural, innate, in opposition to artificial. Certainly in popular language it is used in this restricted sense, as " physical force," signifying bodily force.

The eye of the astronomer, which pierces into the depths of the firmament, must be quenched in darkness; and the brain of the philosopher, which resolves the profoundest problems, must moulder into common dust; the strain of the poet must cease, and his tongue be hushed in the silence of death; all who live must die—the sage and the idiot, the renowned and the obscure! It becomes then a question of the greatest consequence, what is the mental nature of man, and how will death affect it? Has he an immaterial spirit, destined to survive the dissolution of the body, and then enter into another state of existence; or are his mental powers (as the Materialist would urge), merely the results of his physical organization, converging in the brain, and there developing themselves, but which are necessarily dependent upon that organ for their manifestation, and cease to act whenever its mechanism is destroyed? It will be my endeavour to prove the affirmative of this question; viz., that man possesses an immaterial, immortal principle; confining myself however to arguments drawn from Nature and Reason, apart from Revelation. *

Before proceeding, it may perhaps be necessary, in order to prevent confusion, to define the meaning of the terms "Mind" and "Soul" as used in the title of this Essay. I conceive that they are not meant to denote distinct existences or essences; but that they both refer to the same principle; and that the distinction is only made in relation to its different manifestations, and the

---

* These were the conditions proposed by the Northamptonshire Religious and Useful Knowledge Society, for which this Essay was first written.

agreement of the words with the noun-adjectives to which they are joined.

The ancient Greek philosophers employed three terms to denote the vital and mental principle. First, Ζωη or Ζω, signifying life or animation; which was used in common, to designate the vitality of men and brutes. Secondly, Πνεῦμα, signifying breath or respiration; and in a higher sense, by later writers, the spirit or soul. And thirdly, ψυχη, often expressive of an image of the soul (afterwards deified by the Latin Mythologists as Psyche), and spoken of by Homer* as a departed spirit; by Demosthenes and Sophocles† more abstractedly, as the seat of the understanding; by Isocrates, as the disposition, or the seat of the passions or feeling; by others as a living being, a man, and often as a term of endearment, as φιλη ψυχη,— "dear soul." It was also employed to denote a moth or butterfly, from the beautiful transformation of those insects affording a type of the progressive developements of the soul, and its higher nature in a future state.

Among ourselves, the term Mind, is used in popular language, to express the *thinking* faculty, and Soul, the *emotional*. Thus we say, the mind wills, perceives, or reflects; the soul feels, loves, or abhors—the mind judges, reasons, distinguishes; the soul suffers and enjoys, grieves and rejoices, desires and dreads. The mind, as so designated, may be compared to the depths of the ocean—calm, vast, and unfathomable; the soul, to the surface of that ocean—changeful, tossed by storms, and troubled by interrupting agencies, or

---

* Iliad book 23 ver. 65. † Sophocles Elect. 775.

smiling in tranquil beauty, and reflecting the image of heaven. Still, it is the same ocean in both cases. And so I apprehend the thinking and emotional faculties are but different manifestations of the same essence; both constituting that grand element in the nature of man, wherein consists his mental identity. For it were as difficult to perceive how that identity could be preserved in man if he were a duplex being, having two distinct mental natures not referable to one common essence, as that the Siamese twins should constitute one individual.

I propose therefore to use these words in their common acceptation, as referring to the mental nature of man, and shall endeavour to prove that this mental nature is a single, incorporeal, and immortal essence.

The first argument I would adduce in proof of the Immateriality of the Mind, is afforded by considering the nature of the Deity, and by tracing the analogy which exists between God, *as a spirit*, and the *spirit* of man.

Of course neither the Atheist nor the Pantheist will admit this reasoning. Both the man who denies the existence of the Deity, and he who only regards Him as a being identical with Nature, will deny the major of this proposition, viz., that there exists an Infinite Spirit at all. Consequently to such objectors the inference would have no weight. But all who admit that there exists an almighty, omnipresent, infinite, eternal Being, from whom all other beings proceed, and who pervades nature and encompasses it, yet exists independently of and apart from it, grant *that* from which may be deduced inferences tending to prove the Immateriality of the Mind of man. For, I would observe, the nature of the Deity must be immaterial. If the existence of a God is admitted at all, surely it is absurd to suppose Him to be a *physical* Being, resembling a vast Titan, moving from place to place, superintending the spheres, as we might superintend an orrery or a workshop. Such a being, however vast, could only be in one place at a time. There would be bounds to his presence; and all outside that presence must exist apart from him, and be near to, or remote from, his influence. Then instead of being omnipresent, he would be a mere *genius loci*; whereas, throughout nature we receive abundant hints of His ubiquity and His all-pervading influence. But this point need not be further discussed. If there be one thing which nature teaches more than another, it is, that if there be a God, he is an immaterial being, not cognizant to the senses, yet whose presence is universally felt. The star and the daisy; the sun and the sunflower; the ocean and the dew-drop; the hugest and the most minute formations, with organised life in its multifarious forms—in short, everything that surrounds us, as well as we ourselves—attest the presence of a great invisible Spirit,

> "Who gives its lustre to an insect's wing,
> And wheels his flight upon the rolling worlds."

From what the light of nature reveals of the attributes of this Great Spirit, I think he is shown therein to be the Archetype as He is the Author of the human soul, differing from it more in the degree and perfection of those attributes, than in their kind. Nay, further, that there is a greater radical difference in this latter respect, between man and the brute, than between man and God. It is true that as mechanical agents, the inferior animals exhibit wonderful instances of sagacity and skill. The cell of the bee, the nest of the bird, and the storehouse of the ant, have in every age, been regarded as admirable examples of contrivance, and perfect specimens of the best adaptation of means to the end designed. But this very *precision* seems to intimate that they are instinctively, and in a sense passively obeying the dictates of an unerring law, rather than acting as intelligent, thinking, reflecting, beings. Apart from what they are impulsively led to do by their own instinctive powers, their actions betray little that is intellectual. There are no fresh developements,* no strange discoveries, no mental suggestions, no aspiring endeavours. All is tame, precise, stereotyped, calculable, monotonous, *after their kind*—beautifully adapted for the state in which they exist, but shewing or hinting nothing beyond. The human soul, on the contrary, both in its mental and moral constitution, reflects, though dimly and imperfectly, the nature of the Deity. In the intellectual efforts and achievements of man—

---

* I cannot refrain from quoting the following beautiful passage on the subject, from the poet, Montgomery:—
"The Nightingale that sung in Adam's bower,
And poured its stream of music through his dreams;—
The soaring lark that led the eye of Eve
Into the clouds;—
The dove that perched upon the tree of life,
And made her nest among its thickest boughs;—
All the winged inhabitants of Paradise
Whose songs were mingled with the songs of angels,
Built their first nests as curiously and well
As the wood minstrels of our later day."

in his sublime aspirations; in his longings after the infinite; in his vague desires and anticipations; in his power, his skill, his wisdom, his sympathies, his understanding, his sense of justice, of propriety, of virtue; in his love of beauty, and hatred of deformity—in short, in all those things that make up the excellency of his nature—he appears to approximate towards his Divine Original, and faintly shadow His glorious perfections. May we not then justly conclude that as is the Archetype so is the type; as is the sun so is the spark—that if nature abundantly manifests the existence of a spiritual or immaterial being of the highest order, other beings of kindred though inferior powers partake of a nature essentially similar in its kind? This analogy between the greater and the less, may be traced throughout creation. Indeed it is the only method of judging and proving the nature of those things which we cannot grasp or submit to the test of the senses, or of experiment. Thus Franklin inferred that lightning and electricity were identical before he proved the fact by drawing it from the clouds. Thus the chemist analyses a small quantity of common air, and from it deduces the nature of the atmosphere, and its component elements. In like manner he takes a drop of water, and proves from it the nature of the ocean. By this method also the natural philosopher classifies and arranges the various objects that exist, according to the corresponding similitudes or properties he discovers in them. Thus, too, the peasant, who has never seen the ocean, or a greater collection of waters than a pool or small lake, while viewing its miniature phenomena—its tiny billows tossed by the wind; its feeble surges beating against the banks; or its surface, when not disturbed or polluted, imaging the trees that grow upon its side, or the firmament that hangs above it—is convinced that the unknown, unexplored deep is analogous in its nature, although, from what he has heard of it, it is so vastly superior in its manifestations.

May not then, the inference be fairly drawn, that as God is an immaterial Being—judging, contriving, and acting in a most perfect manner, independently of matter—so the mind of man, shewing similar powers, though far more imperfect ones, and possessing a kindred nature, though a far inferior one, (and, alas, how much debased by his own sin and folly!) is immaterial and spiritual also?

Secondly.—The Immateriality of the Mind may be shown from the fact that its qualities, or attributes, are totally unlike the properties or qualities of material things, and that they possess nothing in common.

We know nothing, nor can know anything whatever, of the substratum or essence of any substance, but pronounce on its nature according to the properties or attributes that belong to it. Now, the properties or qualities of matter are of two kinds. First, those that are common, and essential to its nature, which it can never lose, but always retains under every condition, whatever be its transformation—as impenetrability, divisibility, specific gravity, and dimension; and secondly, those that are accidental, which it may retain or lose, according as it may be acted upon—as colour, shape, solidity, size; hardness, softness; roughness, smoothness, and so forth. For example: we take a piece of ice, which we all know to be a cold, solid, brittle substance.

We submit it to the action of increased temperature, when it loses the three former of these properties, and we recognise it as a fluid. Again, by further heat being applied to it, it is converted into the extremely attenuated and elastic vapour which is called steam; which, by the same agency, may be again changed into its component gases. Yet throughout all these transformations we are sure it is the same essence, though appearing in different states, and under different forms, according to the agency which is brought to bear upon it. This is given as a familiar instance, but examples need not be multiplied. The reader is too well acquainted with the various modifications which all things material are perpetually undergoing, and with their different and opposite qualities, to need further illustration.

Now, in no one of these qualities, whether essential or accidental, does the Soul bear any resemblance to material things. To impute to it any of their properties would be preposterous and absurd. It can neither be weighed, divided, nor penetrated, nor has it a tangible form. It is not manifested through the medium of the senses, which is the only way anything material is made known to us. It has neither colour, solidity, size, nor any of the common properties of matter. Fire, wind, and light have, indeed, been sometimes used to furnish representations of it, but merely as poetic tropes, on account of their being subtle and refined in their nature, and the least resembling aught else that is material.

But it must not be supposed that because the Mind possesses no properties in common with matter, that it is, therefore, a mere negation. It has qualities and attributes peculiar to itself, which appear to be the highest manifestations of anything, and the most abiding. I have before hinted at some of these, in tracing the analogy between God and the Soul, and would now more specifically mention them. Metaphysicians have classified them in different ways, and Phrenologists have detailed them with minuteness. But it will be sufficient for my purpose if I briefly refer to the most remarkable. These may be summarily comprehended under the three powers of Volition, Perception and Reflection: those of Volition being the various acts of the Will, as desiring, choosing, etc.; those of Perception, of the Senses, as seeing, hearing, etc.; and those of Reflection, as remembering, judging, reasoning, etc. Now it is obvious that these psychological phenomena are totally distinct from, and unlike any, of the qualities or modifications of matter; as is also the fact that that essence or substance in which they all inhere is simple, and not compound, and incapable of division. If, then, the Mind be regarded as material, do not we act in direct opposition to all principles of classification, and blend into one homogeneous compound things which will not coalesce, and place in one category those things which Nature itself teaches us to distinguish and separate?

But, it may be asked, are we not dependent upon matter for our ideas? And, if so, does not this shew that matter and mind are intimately connected and related?

It has long been a disputed question whether the ideas of the Mind are originally, to some extent, innate, or whether they are all derived through the medium of the senses. I do not intend to enter upon this discussion, for it must be allowed, that if the former theory be the true one, the number of such innate ideas is very limited. But I think this is attributable to the circumscribed state in which the mind is placed, rather than to a deficiency in its capacity; that it is a result of its restriction to this medium of action, rather than because it is unable to act otherwise. In like manner the palate may, owing to circumstances, be confined to tasting only an inferior and course kind of diet, but it is quite capable of relishing different and richer food if such be provided. So the eye of a prisoner is able to take in only a very few objects, and it may be those of the tamest kind, from the loop-holes of his cell; certainly not because of the incapacity of his vision, but on account of his view being thus limited. Throw down his prison walls, or remove him to an eminence, and his sight will range far and wide, among beauties and sublimities before unknown.

The high and active properties of the Mind are also shown by the very ingenious manner in which its primitive ideas are combined by the aid of the fancy, or imagination, until they appear as original conceptions. And also by the reasonings, deductions, and inferences which it is able to draw from whatever is presented to it. And certainly the feelings and emotions of the Soul often seem to rise above material objects altogether. Language is too poor to express them, and affords no medium to convey them to other minds, and no symbol with which to compare them. They are unearthly, unutterable and divine. How often, too, is the body found to be a clog to the soul, and the senses a hindrance to its contemplations! So far from assisting it in its highest thoughts, they only distract and divert it; for it is found that those who are the most attracted by them, and the most eager for their gratification, are amongst the most degraded; while those who abstain as much as possible from sensual pleasures and desires, make the most progress in that which is intellectual. So also those who have lost the use of one or more of the senses, find such loss no obstacle to the exertion of their mental powers. Of this there are many notable examples; for every one must allow that Homer, Galileo, and Milton, thought to purpose without their sight.

We find, therefore, that although the Mind is indebted to sensual or material objects, as furnishing images to supply it with a store of ideas; or, to change the figure, as giving it food to ruminate upon or digest, it is not dependent upon them for its power of acting, neither does it show any affinity to them in its nature.

Thirdly.—The Mind and its phenomena are not referable to material organization.

It is a favourite hypothesis with the Materialist, that mental phenomena are the result of this organization. It has been already noticed that the highest manifestations of Mind, namely, those of the Deity, are not shown in connection with such organization. Why, then, should the human mind result from it? The various contrivances of man, and the different combinations and appliances of his skill, have produced many admirable and surprising results; yet from all the numerous machines which he has constructed, nothing analogous to thought has been developed, unless, indeed, the ingenious calculating apparatus of Babbage may be held to furnish an instance.

The Materialist says it is the *brain* that thinks; that this is its specific function, in the same way as the eye sees and the ear hears. I reply, exactly so: but every physiologist admits that the *eye* does not see; that the *ear* does not hear *per se*, but that they are only *instruments*, for conveying these sensations to the brain or Mind. No one believes that a telescope sees, or an ear-trumpet hears, yet these are only artificial contrivances for extending these senses. We may use them or lay them aside, but the *capacity* remains; and this capacity, in common with other powers of perception, resides in the Mind. If, then, the eye or the ear be only agents or instruments of sensation, why should the brain be regarded as more than the agent or instrument of thought? Can it be the agent and the cause also? If the senses are referable to the brain, must not the brain be referable to something to which *it* also acts as an instrument? If the faculty of vision does not reside in the eye, why should it be supposed that that of thought resides in the brain? The Phrenologist has divided that organ into many distinct, and, I think, somewhat fanciful, partitions, to each of which he assigns specific powers; but supposing this science to be correct in all its minuteness, it only proves that the soul employs a compound instrument instead of a simple one.

A familiar illustration may be given of this. A pianoforte has been beautifully called "a piece of furniture with a soul in it;" but we never suppose the different keys or strings of that instrument to constitute its *music*. That is attributable to a higher, a more ethereal substance, the strings or keys only supplying the medium of action. So the different organs of the brain convey to the Mind the impression made upon them by the world without, and produce those mental effects which may be compared to harmony. And this very naturally accounts for the fact, so strongly dwelt upon by the Materialist, that as the faculties of the body develop themselves, so the mental powers grow stronger, as well as usually decline with its debility and decay. I say *usually,* for there are exceptions sufficient to show that the Mind does not always correspond with the body in this respect, which must have been the case if it were material. But it is generally so found; shewing that, when the latter is deranged or weakened, it acts in like manner upon the former, as a musical instrument, when broken or worn out, sends forth only feeble or discordant sounds.

But it may be objected that matter being visible, or palpable, declares its existence more fully than spirit. But to what is it thus visible or palpable? To itself? Is it matter that thus sees and feels as well as that which is thus seen or felt? To allow this were to reason in a circle—to confound the agent with the subject—that which perceives and knows with that which is perceived and known.

We have more evidence of the existence of Spirit than of Matter. The latter is only made known to us by the perception of the senses, which is sometimes delusive; but the former by conciousness, which is the most satisfactory of all evidence. It is, indeed, curious that any one should doubt the existence of that principle by which he attains the knowledge of the being of any other, and appears as absurd as for a mathematician to doubt the self-evident axioms upon which the whole of his demonstrations rest..

Fourthly.—Another proof of the Immateriality of the Mind is afforded by its identity through all the changes of the physical system.

It is not necessary to enter into any metaphysical discussion for the purpose of proving this identity. We are all convinced of the fact. Our consciousness attests it, and our memory furnishes evidences of it. The man who has lived for fifty or sixty years, knows that he is the same person that he was in youth, in childhood, or in infancy. He can recollect the events of his former life, and never doubts that those events pertain to him as the same individual. Yet it is an ascertained fact that his entire bodily structure has repeatedly changed during that period. There is not a particle of the same matter in his brain, or his heart, or his blood, that there was twenty years back. It is true the change has been very gradual, but it is on that account no less complete. Suppose that from a gallon of sand only one grain be abstracted every hour, and another one placed in its stead. It must be evident that at a given period the whole mass would be as completely changed as if it were done at once. Nor must we confound the resemblance with the identity. It is true the fresh particles of matter are, so to speak, placed in the same mould. The man may retain similar features, a similar tone of voice, a similar gait, &c., (yet in the course of time these peculiarities often greatly alter); but this resemblance no more constitutes his identity than the successive impressions of a printed book constitute it the same copy of that book.

Is it not evident, then, that, if identity does not reside in the Body, it must reside in the Mind?—that there must be something which these corporeal changes do not affect?—an entity that the finger of Time cannot abstract or touch?—that he cannot take away a particle of thought, an atom of will, a molecule of judgment, or a globule of imagination, although he changes the brain piecemeal, and, in a few years, alters the entire bodily man? This argument may be briefly shewn in the following double syllogism:—

That which is changed (whether at once or gradually) cannot remain the same.

But the entire body is imperceptibly changed.

Therefore it is not the same as before that change.

But the mind, being the same is unchanged.

But all that is corporeal (*i.e.*, material) is changed, *ergo*, the Mind must be immaterial.

Did not my limits forbid, I might gather up other evidence in proof of the Immateriality of the Mind, such as the phenomena of sleep and dreaming, the general belief in supernatural agency, and other kindred topics. Nor should I have dwelt so long upon this part of my subject, did I not consider that proofs of the immateriality of our mental nature tell strongly in favour of its immortality also.

For if the Soul be an incorporeal essence, the decay and death of the body will not destroy, but release it. And if sensation reside in it, in common with its other faculties, it will then no longer have to act through a blunted and imperfect medium, but it will be "all eye, all ear, all sense;" perceiving at once those objects of which it is now only dimly and feebly cognizant.

But it must be allowed that the Creator of both matter and spirit could, if He saw fit, annihiliate the soul at any moment, even if it be immaterial; while on the contrary He could continue in perpetual existence matter itself. And so far as our observation goes, He does so continue it; for decay and dissolution must not be confounded with annhiliation, or a tendency towards it. Every organised being undergoes a process of gradual developement, maturity, decay, and dissolution. But this dissolution only precedes fresh forms of life, which, in their turn, undergo the same change. Still we think reason would deduce a termination of being (as far as identity is concerned) from the materiality of the Mind; while the fact of its immateriality—not of necessity sharing the death of the body—furnishes a strong presumptive proof of its surviving that event, and existing for ever.

For I need scarcely stop to remark that the future existence of the soul may be considered as the pledge and promise of its immortality. It is not to be supposed that God, who is unchangeable, would create a soul, and endow it with faculties which are constantly progressing, and powers capable of ever-growing enjoyment, yet capriciously, at some given moment annihilate it. I can discover or conceive of no motive for this in His character as a moral governor, or as an all-wise Being; and, as it has been before stated, nothing is known in the operations of nature anything like annihilation at all. I submit, then, that it may be taken for granted—what few, who believe in a future state of existence, will be inclined to dispute—that, if the Soul exist in a future state, such existence will endure for ever.

On the doctrine of the Immortality of the Soul I need not dwell at length. The subject has often been ably and eloquently discussed. The man is to be pitied whose mind is not convinced, and whose soul is not warmed, by the brilliant pages of those who have discoursed upon this sublime theme—by the glowing fervour of Jeremy Taylor, the classic beauties of Addison, the logical arguments of Butler, the sententious poetry of Young, or the philosophical speculations of Drew or Brougham. Such great and gifted minds have lifted to the imagination the veil which shrouds the invisible world from the sense, and have given us "glimpses that oft makes us less forlorn" while we are imprisoned in this fleshy tabernacle.

The providence of God furnishes a strong argument for the Soul's immortality.

In this world how often are the workings of Providence dark and mysterious! The events which have transspired since the earliest period of history have fully borne out the saying of the inspired Observer, "His ways are in the seas, and His footsteps are not known." How often has the poet lamented the depression of virtue, and the triumph of vice! How do worth and goodness pine in obscurity, while the sordid, the sensual and the selfish are reckoned among the gods of the earth! How does the independent and the deserving mind have to buffet with the difficulties and woes of life, while the worthless and the vile often bask in prosperity and ease! In what inextricable confusion are human affairs often found! How does death appear to be no respecter of persons; or, if he do seem to choose his victims, how often are they among the most worthy, the most useful, or the best beloved! Although we think there is far less inequality in reality than in appearance, in the condition of mankind—that there is a compensating principle in nature which, in no small degree, makes up for the privations and depressions of Fortune; and that Providence is often charged with the evils which are entailed by the follies or vices of men; yet it does appear to require a wider area, and a longer period, to work out its comprehensive scheme and its vast results. Take away the idea of a future state from suffering humanity, and you deprive the sufferer of his greatest panacea; of his chief support; of that which makes his present calamity tolerable; of that hope which is the best antidote to the cup of bitterness which he is obliged to drink! While you add ten-fold to the miseries which encompass him. You extinguish the only gleam of light which shines into the darkness that surrounds him! You increase immensely the difficulties of his position, and efface those divine characters of justice and moral government which are written on every heart! But if at death he is to emerge from this state of privation, suffering, and sorrow, and put on the robes of immortality, the very calamities which he has undergone in this transitory state will add immensely to his felicity. The very contrast will give a keener zest to his enjoyment; and this would appear to be one high reason for the permission of evil at all. Every one knows how sweet health is after sickness, and ease after pain—how a compensation is almost afforded for the sufferings endured. The virtuous will then comprehend why they were made to taste of the bitter waters of life and why it was a state of probation; while they will be far more able to appreciate the happiness to which they have attained, than if they had never suffered at all. The view, too, of the operations of Providence will be greatly extended. Now, only a small segment of the vast circle is visible—the majestic proportions of the plan are lost by the narrow range of the mental vision; but duration and infinity will be for ever unfolding it more fully, and making it more intelligible to the soul!

Again.—The capacities, desires, and aspirations of man require a future life for their full completion and satisfaction.

These sublime wishes and anticipations show the true nobility of our nature. They are also instinctive, and appear to be given us for the highest purposes.

That man betrays a degraded soul, a course and vulgar mind, who is satisfied with present gratifications, and shows no wish beyond them. The highest intellects which have ever appeared, seem to have lived in the past and the future, the distant and the ideal; and to have cherished those divine musings, those "thoughts that wander through eternity," which speculate upon and anticipate a future state. It is the belief in this state which makes the emotions caused by the sublime and beautiful to be intelligible and full of meaning. What are we to undertand by the strange feelings that crowd in upon the soul amidst the grandeur of Alpine scenery, in the depths of the forest, or within view of the ocean? Why the mysterious awe felt upon walking along the dim aisles of a cathedral, or in listening to the solemn anthem swelling along its arches, or echoing from its lofty roof? What mean the grace and beauty of the unrivalled *Venus de Medicis*—" the statue that enchants the world"? Why do we linger over the magnificent pictures of Raphael, or Guido, or Titian? Why does the tragedy of "Macbeth" make the hair stand on end, or "Hamlet" fill the soul with unutterable thoughts? Why are we "never merry when we hear sweet music"? or why does it bear us away as on a seraph's wing? These are all intimations of a nobler, a more spiritual life, pointing onward and upward to it, and are chiefly valuable for the suggestions they afford; and if this life is not to be realised, they are but dark enigmas! empty delusions! cruel mockeries! sublime nothings! tantalizing deceptions!

Scepticism is adverse to literature as well as to devotion, and especially is it fatal to Poetry and the Fine Arts. Indeed, I think it impossible for an Atheist to be a Poet in the highest, the truest, sense of that word. It may suit the worldly, plodding, Utilitarian, to be without a religious creed, but this state is far too cold for the warm imagination of the Bard. Were all his hopes and all his prospects to end in the dreary grave, his harp would be robbed of its sweetest string, and his song would be but an idle sound; but it is because he feels that he has within him a principle that will survive the "wreck of matter and the crush of worlds," that he often attunes his lyre in a strain only inferior to that of the angels above, and antedates the employments of the skies. Is it, then, to be supposed that a God of infinite benevolence would endow his creatures with these capacities and desires, and yet fail to gratify them? Does He do this in any other part of His economy? and would he satisfy the meaner portion of His creation and not the nobler? Are not hints given us every night, from the starry firmament above us, of the boundlessness of His resources and the riches of His universe? Why, then should it be doubted that even we may share in this infinity, and enjoy these riches?

And what heart can conceive the felicity that it is possible for the Soul to enjoy when disembodied, and become a denizen of the skies! If we can now look through the crevices of our fleshly prison, and behold so much that is fair and beautiful, how shall we be enraptured when its walls will be thrown down, and we find ourselves amid grander scenes than the warmest fancy had imagined! If we enjoy so much gratification from dipping into the rill of Truth which meanders through this vale of tears, what unutterable felicity must be experienced by being launched out on its pure and broad waters, which will be perpetually widening and deepening through an infinity of ages!

If what I have been endeavouring to prove be true, how great the responsibility it involves! It is a solemn thing to die; it is a serious thing to live. Perhaps that which most shocks the feelings of all right-minded men, is the flippant, sneering tone in which sceptics, almost without exception, treat the subject of religion and a future state. Scorn is the cant of infidelity, but it is sadly out of place on such topics, and shows bad taste as well as a depraved heart. Such disputations ought surely to be conducted with gravity, and fair legitimate arguments and appeals to the understanding only be used.

Finally.—How thankful ought we to be for the Book of Inspiration, wherein "life and immortality are brought to light"! While endeavouring to pursue this subject by the aid of Reason and the light of Nature alone, the writer felt himself to be groping in the dark, and faintly tracing, in the hieroglyphics of creation, the nature of God and of our own spirits. Neither does he think it possible now to treat this subject altogether apart from the light which Revelation sheds. In reading the opinions of the wisest ancient philosophers as to the nature of the soul, and its destiny, he was much struck with the whimsical and absurd character of many of their notions. Socrates believed in the preexistence of the Soul before birth, as well as its transmigration into that of the brute. Plato, too, was of the same opinion. Indeed, this was the creed of all the most celebrated Grecian philosophers. These profound thinkers, not having the Oracles of Divine Truth, and the light of Revelation to guide them in their investigations, were led astray by the *ignis fatuus* of their own fancy, and could only listen to the voice of their own reason. What wonder then, that they thus erred! But Inspiration now clears up the doubts that have so long enveloped this mysterious subject, and declares, with the voice of God himself, its important truths—

"This is the Judge that stints the strife
Where wit and reason fail"—

Deciding the most embarrassing questions in the simplest manner, and pronouncing the will of God in the plainest words. He that in humility and faith receives this Holy Word, to him will doubtless be given all necessary knowledge; but he that proudly and perversely spurns its teachings, will wander farther and farther in the mazes of error and perplexity, bewildered and lost amidst the mysteries of the universe, and shrouded in its gathering gloom.

The Religious Element in Literature.

A VERY illogical book was some time ago published by a Mr. Birch, M.A., a Materialist, in which the author took immense trouble to prove, from the writings of Shakspeare, that the bard of Avon was nothing more or less than an Atheist—or according to the phraseology of Mr. Birch's school, a Rationalist.*

This attempt, however, signally failed. Every page might be easily confuted, if the book were worth the trouble, but this confutation is unnecessary. It is destined by the momentum of its own stupidity to sink like lead in the waters of oblivion; while the captivating dramas of the mighty poet will be mused over in coming ages, and will still continue to draw the soul into sympathetic union with universal nature, and to elevate and ennoble the mind by teaching it her awful and sublime mysteries. In fact, Mr. Birch's theory is absurd. If Shakspeare had been an Atheist, he had

---

* An Inquiry into the Philosophy and Religion of Shakspeare; by W. J. Birch, M.A., of New Inn Hall, Oxon.—London: C. Mitchell, 1848, p.p. 560.

not been Shakspeare. He could not indeed have been a poet at all.* His efforts would have been paralysed by his unbelief. Poetry and infidelity are quite antagonisic. The dreary creed (if creed it may be called), which disbelieves in a future state, denies the existence of a God, and ignores moral responsibility, is fatal to aesthetics. Of what can such an author write? Of what can such a poet sing? The idea of winning immortal renown whilst the doctrine of immortality is denied, is almost ludicrous, and any attempt at it would be suicidal.

The connection between Literature and Religion is indeed more intimate than may at first sight appear. The religious element is the soul of aesthetics. It pervades, elevates, and ennobles them. It is to them what oxygen is to the atmosphere, or what the atmosphere is to the earth—a life-giving element, whereby this globe is filled with living forms of beauty, and invested with perennial verdure; whilst, lacking this genial influence, all were cold, gloomy, and forbidding, desolation around us, and not a glimpse of the pure heavens beyond. Let us for a moment suppose the religious element to have been by some process abstracted from our Literature—the utilitarian Rationalist to have

---

* It may be objected here that Shelley was an Atheist. Shelley was, however, much better than his creed, if indeed he is to be classed with unbelievers; and his poetry is quite unlike the hard philosophy of Materialists. It is in fact very spiritual in its nature. Shelley's mind was also far from matured. Had he survived his youth, he would probably have forsaken many of his eccentricities. He might have been far from orthodox, but constituted as he was, he could not have been a scoffing sceptic. As it was he was more of a Pantheist than an Atheist.

blotted out every vestige of it from the writings of our standard authors. How have they collapsed! What a dull residuum remains. It is indeed only the dregs of the wine cup from which the exhilarating nectar has evaporated. The disappointed student mourns over his dwindled volumes—folios shrunk to duodecimos, duodecimos to the thinnest pamphlets, pamphlets to a few leaves. But it is not so much the quantity as the quality he laments. The ethereal portion has vanished. Nearly all that has inspired his lonely hours, that has called forth his ardent longings, that has lifted him above the world and its carking cares, that has feasted his soul with mental manna, that has consoled and sustained him in the day of sorrow and of trial, that has heightened the delights of his tranquil and exulting hours, that has invested nature with a meaning and a beauty before unfelt—nearly all this is gone, and the few "wise saws" that remain, are so dry and repulsive, that he would care but little were he to lose them also. What a havoc would this process make with our poets! Milton would vanish in toto, for the mythology he uses, was the religious element of an ancient nation; and though a false system, it proves my statement, as it shows that religion is inherent in the human mind, and abounded in the literature of a people, the most refined upon the face of the earth. But not Milton only, but Young, Cowper, both the Montgomerys, Pollok, Wordsworth, and a whole host of didactic poets, would take to themselves wings and fly away. And others, in whose works the religious element is not so strong and direct,—nay more, those who have been reckoned among the profane, would be shorn of their strength and glory, and would be indeed "of the earth earthy." Byron himself would suffer mutilation; Burns would become a common-place rhymester; and much of that left of Shakspeare, would be like a "tale told by an idiot—signifying nothing." The wild imagination of the "Tempest," the gloomy grandeur of "Macbeth," and the deep philosophy of "Hamlet," are alike unmeaning, except as suggestive of that hereafter which religion makes known. All the supernatural machinery which the poet employs with such thrilling effect, would be forbidden; and even the passions of love, jealousy, avarice, and the rest, so prominently brought out in "Othello," "The Merchant of Venice," "Richard the Third," etc., would lose much of their meaning, and nearly all their interest. It is only as viewed in the light of a future state, that the virtues, vices, and passions of mankind are of sufficient dignity to excite much interest. If there be no hereafter, why the hell in the breast of an Iago?—why the dark despair in the soul of a Macbeth or a King Richard?

Nor would our glorious prose authors fare much better, were their works deprived of this element. Not to speak of the bright galaxy of divines, such as Jeremy Taylor and Howe, Bunyan and Butler, Hall and Chalmers, and a whole host of similar luminaries, who would then lose the whole of their lustre, others in every department of literature—essayists, biographers, novelists, and even historians, would suffer greatly, and be robbed of their distinguishing traits. And were, from this time forth, all authors, whether of prose or verse, to become Rationalists in sentiment, and Infidels in action, how greatly would literature suffer by the change! How contracted would be their field of research; how narrowed their topics; how low and grovelling their thoughts and fancies; how insipid their richest and fairest productions! Literature is indebted to religion for nearly everything in it which is grand, animating or inspiring. What room would there otherwise be for the flights of the imagination? What bard could tune his lyre to the cold philosophy of Materialism, by which matter itself would lose all its spirituality and ideal granduer? The harp of the poet sweeps through the universe, and the notes of his diapason sound loudest in the regions of infinity. Life, death, the grave; eternity, mystery; the soul with its sorrows and aspirations; nature and her deep sympathies and symbols; the unknown and awful future; the ideal and the invisible—these are the themes upon which the poet delights to dwell—the regions he pants to explore. But upon the Infidel chart, these find no place. In its vocabulary, they are words without a meaning; and when referring to them, the Rationalist only treats them as jests, and coldly dismisses them with a sneer.*

It is this religious element in literature which makes it so humanizing in its effects. No poet or true literary amateur can be a ruffian. He may err in many things, and many of his actions may be justly censurable, but he will always be humane. He cannot be charged with beating his wife, or being brutal to his children. His

---

* I must, however, except Holyoake, the most philosophic of the Secularists, who, though a sceptic, is no scoffer, but invariably approaches religious subjects with a gravity which their importance demand. Would that other freethinkers would copy his spirit in this respect.

vices are, indeed, likely to take an opposite character. He may be profligate, but he will be kind-hearted; he may be indiscreet, but he cannot be severe; he may be voluptuous, but he cannot be vulgar; he may be vain and selfish, but he cannot be cruel. The deep communion which he holds with nature, and the strong sympathy which he feels with every sentient being, utterly forbid any callousness to take possession of him, whilst the high and holy subjects of his contemplation implant a kind of natural piety in his soul, and he is led upwards from nature to nature's God. I do not mean to assert that this is religion, or that it will be found a valid substitute for it, but it is of great use as far as it goes, to soften, humanize, and refine its possessor, and, on this account, is very valuable to society.

In conclusion, I would just observe that this strong intimacy between literature and religion, affords striking evidence of the truth of the latter. The Divine Giver of all good (or if the infidel please, our bounteous mother Nature) would surely never give us these divine and ardent longings and aspirations, if we are not destined to realise them. Are the budding wings of the chrysalis to be for ever confined within the shell? Do not they rather betoken that their possessor will soon emerge from its wintry prison, and wanton unconfined in the boundless expanse of air? Does not nature sooner or later satisfy the desires of every living thing? Is not provision made for the instincts and capacities of every animal, however low in the scale of being? And shall man, the masterpiece of the creation, the crowning excellency of earth, be alone doomed to disappointment? Must he go to his long home, with his high and holy instincts and aspirations ungratified, or with his growing capabilities for ever blighted, merely to feast the worm? Nature with her thousand voices utters an emphatic "No"; and the utterances of his own soul, and the delights he has experienced in communing with the souls of others who have set forth in their literary labours the grandeur of the human intellect, alike echo the prophetic exclamation.

Death.

(WRITTEN IN THE AUTUMN).

THE autumnal season naturally leads the mind to the contemplation of death. Its falling leaves and decaying vegetation; its moaning winds, sounding like a wail from the spirit-world; its shortening days, gloomy skies, and obscure fogs, causing nature to appear as though she were to about return to her pristine state of chaos and darkness; the gathering cold and damp, making one to shudder, and feel the frailty of the human frame;—all these, and the other characteristics of the season, like so many monitors, join in the solemn warning, "Son of man, thou too, art mortal! Like all things beneath the moon, thou must decay—thou must die!" I propose, very briefly, to offer a few reflections on this trite, but important and deeply suggestive subject, hoping that the hints I throw out may be of some service in the calm study of the *"philosophy of death."*

First.—Death is an inevitable law of our nature. All must obey it, and it therefore becomes us to obey it cheerfully. We are sure that where perfect wisdom is the lawgiver, the law must be good, though to our narrow view it may appear an evil. Granted that it is the fruit of sin, and is meant as a punishment for transgression; still Infinite Wisdom knows how to educe good from evil, as He has done in ten thousand instances. We may see a little of its beneficial tendency in its universality. Suppose some were exempt, and like the fabulous "Wandering Jew," were to live on to the end of time. Would the reader like to be one of those *athanatoi ?* Would he not be isolated from his kind, in a dreary and forlorn solitude, the prey of *ennui*, and without human sympathy or human fears? There are moments when one looks to death as the mariner to his haven—as the shipwrecked voyager to his wished-for port of refuge—as the banished, to a reunion with his long-lost loved ones—as the weary traveller to his home. At other times, an irresistible curiosity is felt to pierce the mysterious veil which separates us from the spiritual state, and hides the wondrous vision. We long to learn the nature of that high destiny to which our instincts, powers, and aspirations tell us we may attain ;—to know something of those serene orbs which, whilst in the flesh, tantalize us nightly with their solemn beauty, and bewilder us with their amazing distances, size, and number. We would fain get some knowledge of this after-state, even at the expense of dying to realise it. Moreover, death acts kindly in putting a speedy end to the sufferings and infirmities of our nature; in thwarting pride and tyranny; in rebuking vanity and arrogance; and in levelling those distinctions of social life which would otherwise render our existence loathsome and intolerable. "There the wicked cease from troubling, and the weary are at rest; there the prisoners rest together, they hear not the voice of the oppressor. The small and the great ones are there, and the servant is free from his master." Job iii. 17, 20.

Secondly.—The instinctive dread of death is wisely ordained. Just suppose this dread to be not so great as it is, or that it were not dreaded at all. The present economy of life would be thwarted. Men would escape from their griefs and miseries by continual acts of suicide. Even now, strong as is the dread of death, painful as the act of dying is supposed to be, awful as is the guilt of self murder, cases of suicide are constantly occurring; and we learn from history, that at some periods, the mania was alarming, almost threatening the extinction of society. How much more would it be increased were this instinctive dread to be weakened or extinguished! If, instead of being in a high degree repulsive, it were to be as pleasant as going to sleep, or as little thought of as stepping from one room to another, it is manifest that there would be no security nor confidence. Society would be speedily disorganized and broken up, and the human race would soon come to an end. The instinctive fear of death is the great preserver of life; and the principle is wisely decreed to be as strong and perpetual in its operation as the impulse which secures the perpetuity of our race. Still it is to be desired that this instinct should be healthy and not morbid. Many "through fear of death, are all their life-time subject to bondage." An oversensitive nervous organization destroys their happiness, by miserable anticipations of the hour of their dissolution.

Often it is dying, rather than death, that is feared; and sometimes a sickly fancy afflicts itself by pourtraying the horrors of the grave—the narrow coffin with the earth rattling upon it—the silence of the tomb and its gloomy obsequies! Both these terrors will often fly before a calm philosophic inspection of them. With respect to the first, it is believed by many of our ablest physicians that the bodily pain endured in the act of dying (if act that can be called, which is often nearly passive) is trifling, and that frequently the patient is without nervous sensibility altogether. The convulsions and distortions which appear so frightful, are merely spasmodic affections of the nerves of motion, which are entirely distinct from those of feeling, the latter being frequently dormant in a dying person. It is in previous stages of the disease that the greatest bodily agony is experienced; as pain is like a sentinel who quits his post when no longer of use. As to the horrors of the grave itself, and its gloomy paraphernalia, it is obvious upon reflection, that the sufferer is terrified by a morbid imagination which is altogether delusive. He supposes the corpse to become conscious, to be in fact *himself*; whereas he will cast it off like a worn-out garment, until re-united at the general resurrection. At the same time it must be admitted that many of our ideas, as to the repose of the tomb, the undisturbed quiet of the grave, and similar phrases in common use, are illusory in a similar way. The soul does not necessarily rest, because the body is lying quiet; neither may it have found a haven of peace, because its partner is reposing undisturbed within the tomb. The individual vexed with the cares and storms of life, often passes the grave-yard and envies those that are sleeping within its quiet precincts, forgetful that it contains only their ashes, and that the immortal spirit has gone to "give an account of the deeds done in the body, whether they be good or whether they be evil," and to be "rewarded according to its works."

Lastly.—The nature of a future state has been very properly concealed. Here again, suppose the contrary to have been the fact. Suppose all knew the destiny of the soul after death, and as much of the after state, as of the new world which Columbus discovered. A moment's reflection will shew that it would absorb all our attention, and that we should not be in a position to attend to the duties, cares, or pleasures of life. A fugitive state like the present would indeed have few cares. We should pass it as one passes the vestibule of a temple, intent upon the splendours or grandeurs that meet the eye from within. There is just enough revealed to engage our attention, but not to engross it. I have sometimes heard it said "we should always live as if the present day was our last." I cannot agree with this sentiment. A man who believes he is going to die to-morrow, is not likely to discharge the duties or enjoy the pleasures of to-day. Providence has very wisely left the time of our death a secret; and also, for a similar reason, has kept unrevealed the nature of an after existence. Still, as death is a certain and inevitable event, which may at any moment take place, it becomes all to contemplate it with thoughtful seriousness, and to prepare to meet it with calmness and dignity, if not with confidence and joy.

I would conclude this paper by recommending to the

reader a beautiful poem, on the subject of death, by Bryant, an American bard, entitled, "Thanatopsis," from which I quote the closing verses:—

> "So live, that when thy summons comes to join
> The innumerable caravan, that moves
> To the pale realms of shade, where each shall take
> His chamber in the silent halls of death,
> Thou go not, like the quarry-slave at night,
> Scourg'd to his dungeon; but sustain'd and soothed
> By an unfalt'ring trust, approach thy grave,
> Like one who wraps the drapery of his couch
> About him, and lies down to pleasant dreams."

Common Sense
VERSUS
Transubstantiation.

EVERY one who values aright the deductions of reason, must be aware that they are based upon certain self-evident axioms, or elementary principles, which cannot be called in question, but which must be taken for granted at the outset of every logical dispute or affirmation. To deny them, is to act contrary to the dictates of common sense, and is in fact to throw overboard the rudder of human reason, and to give up the certain and the positive, for the false and contradictory. It is wisely ordained that they strike the mind at once, and need no proof; and are placed at the very threshold of knowledge, so that he who stumbles at any one of them can never enter its divine precincts, but lies prostrate at its porch, the miserable votary of unbelief or superstition. It is here that the extremes of incredulity and credulity meet together, for it is generally found that some one or other of the simple fundamental truths to which I allude, is tacitly or openly rejected, in order to make way for a monstrous and absurd dogma—the gnat is strained at, that the camel may be swallowed. The simple elementary axioms to which I refer are of this nature:—That a part cannot be greater nor so great as the whole; that no substance can be in two places at the same time; that two straight lines can never approach each other; that two and two are equal to four at all times and in all places; that a thing cannot change and remain the same; that every effect must have a cause, etc. Some of these axioms may be termed mathematical, others geometrical, others metaphysical, but they are all related to each other in this respect—that their contraries express a physical absurdity, because impossibility, or that which we are assured *can never be,* and which therefore the reason rejects. I would remark here that a mystery ought never to be confounded with a natural impossibility. This is often done; but a little investigation will show the difference between them.

A Mystery is such, owing to our limited powers of apprehension or comprehension; and the more insight we have into its true nature, the more it brightens up before the mental vision, until it is a mystery no longer. But a natural impossibility is as absurd and contradictory (or more so) to the most penetrating or subtle intellect, as it is to the ignorant clown. The science of astronomy affords a striking proof of the former. What is a greater mystery to the uninitiated than the method by which worlds are weighed as in a balance—their distances accurately measured, their true motions nicely detected, or their size revealed? And yet when the mind is instructed in this exact science, the mystery gradually vanishes, and the method becomes clear and manifest. Not so, however, the latter. Its nature is still as contradictory to the philosopher as to the peasant, and greatly more absurd; nay, had we the powers of an angel we may be sure that we should get no nearer towards ridding it of its contradictory character. It is not a little remarkable that neither in Nature nor Revelation (save the doctrine under dispute) is the mind ever called upon to believe in what appears to be a manifest physical impossibility. There are many things in both which are profoundly mysterious, and which perhaps the human mind will never thoroughly fathom. Of this kind are Eternity, Infinitude, the nature of the Deity, the nature of Being in general, the principle of Life, the resurrection of the dead, etc. But it is manifest that this is not owing to the nature of these things in themselves, but to our own limited powers. There is nothing in them which shocks or does violence to the intellect; on the contrary, it is just what might be expected, since the less cannot contain the greater, nor is it likely that man, "born like the wild ass's colt," should be able to comprehend the universe. There is much, it is true, about eternity and infinity which *appears* contradictory, but the mind almost intuitively and instinctively knows that this is only in appearance; whereas the things mentioned above, involve contradictions which the mind as instinctively rejects.

Now a system of religion which imposes any one of these contrarieties, must of necessity, so far, rest on a false basis. It may be *a priori* regarded as an imposture, although, upon further research and acquaintance, many truths may be found mixed up with it. It was in this way that Islamism and the hoary system of Oriental mythology fell before the introduction of a pure philosophy. The absurd tenets intertwined with these faiths would not bear the light of true science, and are therefore now not seldom laughed at by their own priests and nominal adherents. The absurdity, however, of believing in the doctrine of transubstantiation is greater than this, since it becomes glaring to the dictates of common sense; whereas in the other case it is only apparent by the profound deductions of science.

Let us then briefly test this doctrine by the principles I have laid down. *It cannot be* that a body can be in two places at the same instant, and yet Popery teaches that the body of Christ is in heaven, at the same time that it is received into the mouth of the communicant, and that His blood is flowing in His sacred veins whilst it is simultaneously being elevated in the priest's chalice; and the priest declares he dare not administer it to the vulgar laity *lest they should spill a drop of the divine ichor*. *It cannot be* that two and two are more or less than four at all times and in all places, or that a part is greater than the whole, and yet Popery teaches that the material body of Christ is divided into innumerable wafers, and exists at once in Italy, in France, in Britain, in America, and elsewhere, which collectively would make many such bodies of the size of common humanity, and as His when upon earth. Surely, without irreverence, we may say that he who can believe this, would not scruple to believe as great an absurdity as that of Jonah swallowing the whale. It is in vain to explain the thing away by speaking of a *sacramental* presence, which conveys no idea to the mind, and is only therefore a phrase without meaning; or a *spiritual* presence, since spirit is not body, and therefore this dogma also involves a contradiction in terms.

Foreshadowings.

IF a person on opening a book were to find interwoven with the text the word "tobacco," he might rest assured, beyond all doubt of controversy, that the book was written after the close of the fifteenth century. In this way many works of assumed antiquity have been tested, and disputations concerning them set at rest. Still, such inferences should not be too hastily drawn, or the judgment may be led astray, especially if the phrases leading to the specific conclusion be common ones, incorporated with the language, and having different significations.

This thought was suggested by my taking up at random a volume of poems, and alighting by chance on the following couplet—

"Slumbers *and hears by starts the noisy train;*
"Catches a period, and drops down again."

Now where does the reader suppose this verse is to be found? "Of course" I hear him reply, "in some poem written subsequently to the era of railways; for forty years ago, they must else have been used by a prophet, and would have appeared darkly enigmatical if not sheer nonsense." It is a fact however that the couplet is near a century old, and appears in the 72nd page of the third volume of Dodsleys' collection of poems, a miscellany published in the year 1775, the specific piece being "The Mimic," composed by a Rev. Mr. Pitt, probably a relative of the "heaven-born minister." A glance at the poem will show the discerning reader that the "noisy train" does not refer to our iron locomotives, but to the retinue of a court of law; and yet there is little or nothing in the passage itself, or its context, tending to confute some wiseacre of a thousand years hence, who should endeavour to prove from it, either that railways were in use prior to the last century, or that the poem itself was composed subsequently to the year 1830. We know that such conclusions have been drawn by ignorant and superficial persons, one of the most curious being that of Joe Smith, the founder of Mormonism, who, not dreaming of any anachronism, seriously lays it down that St. Paul's vessel was steered by the mariners' compass, because the narrative says "we *fetched a compass*, and sailed to Rhegium."—(Acts xxviii, ver. 13.)

The above may be regarded as singular instances of accidental coincidence; but there are others to be found in our current literature of so curious a character as almost to justify the idea of their being regarded as presentiments, or foreshadowings of circumstances, discoveries, or inventions, about to follow or to be revealed. It is as though the authors of them—generally poets —laid claim to their ancient character of "seers," and in their sublime reveries had glimpses of what was to come to pass in after days. I would instance two or three as they recur to my own mind.

In that weird-like poem, "The Ancient Mariner," is the following singular passage:—

"FIRST VOICE.
"But why drives on that ship so fast
"Without or wave or wind?
"SECOND VOICE.
"The air is cut away before,
"And closes from behind."

Now when it is considered that these verses were written in the first decade of the present century, before steamships or atmospheric railways were heard of, it is I think not preposterous to suppose that the gifted author had some dim presentiment of the practical application of steam and hydraulic power about to be called forth to revolutionise the world.

The boast of Puck, in the "Midsummer Nights' Dream,"—

"I'll put a girdle round about the earth
In forty minutes,"

has, since the invention of the electric telegraph, been so often quoted in connection with it, that any further mention of it is well-nigh superfluous. The most curious circumstance is that science has here out-done the wild fancy of a poet gifted beyond all others in inventive powers; and almost realizes the extravagant invocation that Nat Lee puts into the mouth of one of his characters—

"Ye Gods annihilate both space and time
And make two lovers happy."

There are in the Spectator, and scattered up and down other of the British classics, passages regarded as anticipatory of the march of invention, of which I will only instance the story of the Rosicrucian Sepulchre, to be found in No. 379 of the Spectator, bearing the appropriate motto "Science is not science until revealed."

"A certain person having occasion to dig somewhat deep in the ground, where the philosopher, Rosicrucius, lay interred, met with a door having a wall on each side of it. His curiosity, and the hopes of finding some hidden treasure, soon prompted him to open the door. He was immediately surprised by a sudden blaze of light, and discovered a very fair vault. At the upper end of it was a statue of a man in armour, sitting by a table, and leaning on his left arm. He held a truncheon in his right hand, and had a lamp burning before him. The man had no sooner set one foot within the vault, than the statue erected itself from its leaning posture, stood bolt upright; and upon the fellow's advancing another step, lifted up the truncheon in his right hand. The man still ventured a third step, when the statue with a firm blow broke the lamp into a thousand pieces, and left his guest in a sudden darkness.

Upon the report of this adventure, the country people soon came with lights to the sepulchre, and discovered that the statue, which was made of brass, was nothing more than a piece of clock-work; that the floor of the vault was made all loose, and underlaid with several springs, which, upon any man's entering, naturally produced that which had happened.

"Rosicrucius, say his disciples, made use of this method to show the world that he had re-invented the ever burning lamps of the ancients, though he was resolved no one should reap any advantage from the discovery."

Now whether the "ever-burning lamps of the ancients" had a real existence or not, may be doubted; but I think a person reading the account in the middle of the nineteenth century cannot but be struck with its applicability to the gas lamps of the present day, which have realised the fable, and rendered abortive the labour of Rosicrucius to conceal the discovery.

It is a curious fact that the light which the science of the present century sheds, brings out into bold relief, and intensifies certain phrases of our old poets, beyond any possible meaning they could have had when written, either to the author or to the reader. I conceive this to be the case with the closing line of the following quaint and forcible sonnet by Thomas Randolph, a Northamptonshire poet, which I am sure the reader will pardon my quoting entire:—

"TO MY PICTURE.

"When age hath made me what I am not now
And every wrinkle tells me where the plough
Of time hath furrow'd; when an ice shall flow
Through every vein, and all my head be snow;
When Death displays his coldness in my cheek,
And I, myself, in my own picture seek,
Not finding what I am but what I was;
In doubt which to believe, this or my glass;
Yet, though I alter, this remains the same
As it was drawn; retains the primitive frame
And first complexion; here will still be seen
Blood on the cheek and down upon the chin:
Here the smooth brow will stay, the lively eye,
The ruddy lips, and hair of youthful dye:
Behold what frailty we in man may see,
Whose *shadow* is less given to change than he!"

Now the reader will observe that if an ancient portrait, drawn by a limner, may be called a shadow—and it may without any violence to the word—how much more forcibly does the term apply to a modern photograph, which is the literal shadow of the person it represents!

Great men, as events have testified, have not unfrequently been endowed in some degree with the power of prescience—of foreshadowing, and of anticipating events and conditions of society unlike those of their own day—of projecting themselves into the future, and often becoming the harbingers of better times. Thus it was with Milton, who in his treatise on the Liberty of Unlicensed Printing, eloquently descants on the time visible to his mind's eye, when the press—that mighty engine of civilization—should be untramelled, and the nations should bask in the sunshine of liberty. Watt and Stephenson, too, though laughed at as crazy projectors, foretold the triumphs of steam. And I think few can now read Burke's Reflections on the French Revolution, without being struck with the singular confirmation of his practical conclusions with the event, even in remote and minute particulars.

With respect to future times, there appears to be one poet now living among us, who if I mistake not, is gifted to a remarkable degree with the power of foreshadowing. I refer to Alfred Tennyson, the laureate. Much of his poetry is fired with prophetic anticipations of a glorious future for mankind, when the law of continual advancement will be fully developed. He loves to herald this bright era, for which advent creation has groaned and travelled through the ages, and is himself a

"Voice in the rich dawn of an ampler day."

This bright anticipation is especially the burden of "Locksley Hall," in which he speaks of hope for sinning and suffering humanity, and sings the song of progress like a man inspired. Whether or no the inventive genius of our race will take the precise turn that he predicts may be doubted, but if posterity do not realise aerial argosies, dropping down their rich bales, or atmospheric battle-ships plunging into the clouds, making strange thunder, and shedding ghastly dews of blood, there is but little doubt that the "younger day" of brotherhood, peace, and harmony, will eventually dawn upon the world, and that science in a thousand ways is helping onward the glorious epoch.

The Uses of Poetry.

I AM not one of those who are always crying out *cui bono?* and form a rather mean opinion of the Utilitarian. I think too that an answer might easily have been given to the practical man who objected to Milton's "Paradise Lost," by putting the question "what does it prove?" Prove, my friend, why it proves much. It proves that we have had at least one man among us capable of fascinating the noblest natures throughout every succeeding age, with his wondrous power of song. It proves the grandeur of the human intellect; the power of Mind, that can lay under tribute worlds unseen; the attributes of Imagination that can plunge into abyssmal depths, and soar to empyreal heights—can awe us with ghostly terrors, or delight us with angelic glories; it proves the force of Genius that can chant the song of creation with the morning stars, and tell the sublime story of our race with almost the power and pathos of an angel. It proves the reality of these endowments. And is all this to be reckoned of no account—of no comparative value, when placed by the side of a mathematical solution, a physical discovery, or a mechanical invention? All honour to those brave natures who have toiled and moiled through many weary years for the practical advancement of their fellows in civilization and power; but let us not hold in too low an estimation, or give quite away, those men of still higher endowments, who have proved the nobility of our common nature, and who delight throughout all time those cultivated and elevated minds that can appreciate their genius.

And if this may be said *par excellence* of one of the grandest poems that have ever been penned, it may also in a subordinate degree be affirmed of poetry in general. Poetry may be especially valued as a humaniser, an elevator, and an interpreter. If there be one class of persons more than another who ought to welcome and cherish poetry, and thank God that they can feel and appreciate it, it is the working class. This divine gift is in no way exclusive; it often passes by the mansions of the great and the wealthy, to alight with all its sweet influences on the cottages of the poor and lowly. And not only does it soften and smooth their hard and angular lot, and enhance the enjoyments of humble life, but where cherished, it always humanises and refines its possessor. A poet, or a lover of poetry, must of necessity be a man of feeling; to be cruel or brutal would be contradictory to his nature. A young woman who marries such an one, may at least reckon upon being safe from brutality. Her husband may have faults, and his faults may degenerate into crimes, but she may ever cherish the consoling assurance that as long as he is in a sane state of mind, his sensibility will be a sufficient guarantee against his ill-using her by that cowardly cruel treatment which is so often inflicted upon her poor suffering sisterhood, by ignorant sensual men. The hand employed in writing a poem, never was or can be lifted aginst a feeble woman; and the tongue that can voice its utterances with real feeling, can never wound and insult her with coarse maledictions.

Poetry is a precious boon, which opens the heart, refines the soul, and expands the intellect—a heavenly guest, which asks for admission by appealing to the sensibilties of our own nature, which whoever entertains, will find that an angel has crossed his threshold unawares! It is a kind of natural piety, that draws the heart towards the fount of excellence, and purifies and ennobles the affections. It reveals the solemn grandeur of our nature and destiny, and teaches its possessor that he has the power of rising higher and still higher in the scale of existence, brightening his pathway as he climbs the sublime eminence, until he "summers high in bliss upon the hills of God." It teaches him the sublime law of universal brotherhood, and shows him that "one touch of nature makes the whole world kin." It calls forth an universal sympathy with nature—not only with the sublime and magnificent, but with the simple and the lowly, which others stay not to regard, or else heedlessly overlook.

The lover of poetry cannot view the "meanest flower that blows," without it suggesting to him "thoughts that lie too deep for tears;" and while others are pursued by *ennui*, or scared by solitude, he revels in thick-teeming fancies, and delights in "dainty melancholy." His imagination (almost creative in its energies) is ever suggesting new ideas. Nature is his kaleidescope which he can shift at will—always forming new, strange, and startling combinations, to delight his soul and instruct him in the boundless capabilities of his nature, and in the bounteous provision so exquisitely designed for it, which he finds sown broadcast through the earth and heavens, blooming in every flower, and beaming from every star.

Poetry is an Interpreter. Nature is full of symbols—of dark enigmas, which it is the high prerogative of Genius to explain. On the contrary, it may well be said of the prosaic matter-of-fact person:—

> "A primrose by the river's brim,
> A yellow primrose is to him,
> And it is nothing more."

But the poet finds in it a hidden meaning, and a beauty which he feels, but can never fully express. He knows *why* the lily is fair, and the rose beautiful; those simple flowers being to him types of the eternal forms of purity, grace, and lovliness in the soul. The symbolic character of Nature in all her multiform appearances affords him curious and recondite topics of meditation, and hints of an ever-developing system of infinite progress and exaltation.

It is a gratifying fact that the great storehouse of poetry is alike open to all—to the poorest as well as to the richest of the human family. There are many studies that require considerable outlay before they can be pursued to advantage; but not so this study. The rich treasures which the poet needs, are provided by the munificent hand of Nature herself, and are dealt out in common to all those who wish to regale themselves at her banquet. Although the poet may not possess an inch of land he can call his own, and his purse be as lean as his person, still to his enjoyment, the riches of the universe are tributary; for him the stars, millions of leagues distant, pour their flood of glory; and he can extract from the sunshine and the shade, the mountains and the rivers, the flowers, the brooks, and the birds, an infinitely greater enjoyment than the rich sensualist can find in viewing his broad acres, and riding over his spacious domains. Let not then the sons of Genius complain that they are in a state of poverty—that they are unpatronised and neglected. They may smile at the rich man's scorn and the proud man's contumely, since they can find enjoyment in communing with Nature and their own minds, which must afford them unceasing intellectual gratification, and will amply repay them for suffering and privation. Let them not repine because they cannot command the paltry pleasures of earth; since they can partake of the food of angels and the luxury of the skies.

POEMS.

"———NOTING ERE THEY FADE AWAY,
"THE LITTLE LINES OF YESTERDAY."

ROGERS.

The Dirge of Nature.

As some swift river with increasing force,
   Noiseless and unobstructed rolls its way,
For ever bearing in its downward course
The glittering straws that on its surface play;
So Time is hastening all things to decay—
The worldling's treasure and the monarch's crown;
Each, like the fleeting pageant of a day
Fades, as his passing breath is o'er them blown,
And domes and pyramids are by his touch o'erthrown!

I sat with Desolation on the tower—
The mouldering tower that crumbles 'neath the sky—
And as he stretch'd his iron hand in power,
I saw in vision, ages rolling by;—
Each like a mighty billow met mine eye,
Onward impell'd by every following wave,
'Till in Eternity's wide sea they die,
Each bearing generations to the grave—
The affluent and mean, the coward and the brave!

The eve of time before my vision rose
   In silent pomp. The sons of Mirth had fled;

Hush'd was the wail of melancholy woes;
For all were slumbering with the quiet dead—
All, save a solitary form, whose tread
Was noiseless, as o'er many a grave he stray'd;
It seem'd old Adam's ghost, by fancy led
To haunt the places where his sons were laid,
And view the mounds of Death the Spoiler's hand had made.

But 'twas a spirit wrapp'd in mortal clay—
A lonely minstrel, last of human mould;
Around his hoary locks the parting ray
Of sunlight play'd, and sportive breezes roll'd,
While his whole form seem'd venerably old,
And at his side a harp depending, hung,
Whose strings he swept as o'er the graves he prowl'd,
And Nature's solitary requiem sung,
While echo far around, the solemn music flung.

The Minstrel touch'd his lyre :—
"Oh dying sun!
"What mean those burning forms that round thee fly?
"Are they commission'd when thy race is run,
"To hurl thee downward from the lofty sky,
"To depths unfathomable, there to die?
"For thou art setting now to rise no more!
"And like the pillowy clouds that 'neath thee lie,
"Wilt drop away and perish, and thy store
"Of burning beams will fade, by darkness cover'd o'er!

"O! linger yet, and kiss the mountain tops;
"Diffuse thy parting radiance far around;—
"This awful hour the wheel of Nature stops,
"And all is lost in reverie profound!

"Time pauses! silence reigns! nor wandering sound,
" Nor sighing gale, nor murmur, breaks the gloom;—
" Nature is waiting for her final wound;
" Ready for Destiny to seal her doom,
" And roll her vast domains into Oblivion's tomb!

" Where now the ages past—the eras fled?
" Like dreams when one awakes, they seem to be;
" Or like huge rocks which from the mountain's head
" Are cast, and buried 'neath the rolling sea;—
" Sunk in the ocean of eternity,
" Are days, and years, and ages; all are gone!
" With what amazing swiftness did they flee,
" Propell'd by Him who sits upon His Throne
" And bids Eternity's wide circling wheel roll on!

" My lyre thy notes renew—a sacred song—
" Palmyra's ancient dust demands thy strains—
" That city which from distant ages, hung
" In haughty ruins mid' forsaken plains!
" Tell, tell the winds, what remnant now remains,
" Or spoil, where poetry may build her dreams;
" Is there no fane, what time the cold moon wanes,
" That echoes lonely plaints, and fearful screams,
" Or now lifts high its head to catch the sun's last beams?

" Proud Balbec fell, but not alone she fell;
" Her ruins spread their leaven all abroad,
" And Gallia's city fled; and her sad knell
" Was echo'd long, and sea-girt Britain heard;
" As Time pass'd by he gave the potent word,
" And lo! her strength departed, and her pride,
" Bow'd to the dust, no more its head uprear'd,

" But round her shores mad billows now deride,
" And taunting, ask her waste what splendour she en-
    joy'd !

" But lo ! the sun is set—for ever set !
" Gone to his death-bed underneath the skies !
" For lively scenes, dark gloominess instead
" Must hang o'er all, for morn will ne'er arise !
" Ye heavens, how are ye taken by surprise !
" Soon must the planets from their orbits fall !
" The weary moon rises in blood and dies !
" Hang out ye skies the universal pall,
" And let cimmerian darkness overspread you all.

" And let my strain be hush'd ;—why wanders now
" Upon the margin of eternity,
" My feeble song, when all above, below,
" Around, in one deep, solemn silence, lie !
" The stars have ceased their dances round the sky ;
" The winds no longer rock the sleeping dead ;
" No more o'er ocean's face the billows fly ;
" But all in loneliness and night is laid ;
" So shall my strain be hush'd, and wandering harp be
    stayed !"

Lyra Mortis:

AN ODE.

UPON the deadly Upas tree,
    Which man, and beast, and bird must flee;
Which, whereso'er its influence spreads,
Poison contaminating sheds,
And like a tyrant with fell breath,
Lives but to bid all creatures die,
Feasting on human misery;—
There hung the harp of Death!

The bony monster plac'd it there,
    And gave a ghastly grin;
It was strong with sinews stout and bare,
Torn from the dead which in heaps lay there,
    And its sound was a heavy din!
Hark, now it floats on the struggling breeze!
The fingers of Death are sweeping the lyre;—
He calls on his train, and the wide-spreading plain
    Is throng'd with phantoms dire;—
The DISEASES that prey on the great and the small,
They haste, they haste, at their monarch's call!

They come, a ghostly band,
Each from a distant land;
Their hollow voices babbling on the air—
　　　Screams and cries,
　　　Groans and sighs,
　　　Sounds of woe,
　　　Moanings low,
And wild delirious tones of phrensy and despair!
　　Summon'd by their terrific king,
　　They come the lyre to sound—
　　Eager to strike each trembling string,
　　And make the plains resound.

But who is he, pressing in front of the crew,
With locks all dishevell'd, that sport on the blast?—
See his eyes, how they're glaring so fiercely and blue!
He gnashes his teeth, and moves wildly and fast.

'Tis MADNESS: in haste he snatches the lyre,
And sweeps its dread chords with impetuous ire,
For a storm's at his heart, and his brain is on fire!

　　Appall'd the scared Diseases stand,
　　And listen to his notes,
　　Far, far away, to regions bland,
　　The music wildly floats!

He sung of the mad moon hurrying by,
And the tempest that low'rs in the darkened sky;
Of dizzying heights, and of gaping graves;
Of desolate rocks, and of splashing waves;
Of furies, with snakes in their twisted hair,
And of cold and motionless Despair!
Then he stray'd from his theme, and a cooling tear,
Stole down his cheeks, and he sung of love;—

Quite tender and slow did his notes now flow,
And he seemed surcharg'd with grief and woe,
    And cast his eyes above.

A cloud was sailing along the sky;
It was silvery white and it caught his eye,
And he fancied it wafted his Love away,
Whose ashes were wrap'd in the cold, cold clay;
And he held out his hand in the empty air,
And as tranquil a smile as he used to wear,
'Ere grief had distracted his raging breast,
Play'd on his face, and his heart seem'd at rest.
And he sung of his Love in the bright, bright bower,
Where they used to stray in the moon-lit hour;
For so potent the spell that entranc'd him then,
He seem'd to enjoy her sweet presence again.
It vanish'd—the cloud that pictured her form,
Evanescent yet fair on the verge of the sky,
No longer by billowy breezes up-borne—
Sunk, fled like a dream from his languishing eye.
Then a wild fit of phrensy came over his soul,
Nor effort nor force could his fury control;
But he hurried his fingers along the dread lyre,
And deafening music burst forth from each wire—
Deep as his passion, and strong as the power
That onward impell'd him in that fated hour,
And loud as the thunder that rolls in the sky—
While lightnings fierce flash'd from the maniac's eye!
Then abruptly he ceas'd; his wild harpings were o'er,
And away to the verge of the mountains he tore;
Then with a mad laugh, and a loud piercing yell,
Down, down, in the wide yawning chasm he fell!

He fell—as when imperial Jove
Hurl'd Mulciber from heaven above ;—
A silence midst his host was found,
Stricken with terror, and spell-bound ;—
So the Diseases stood in reverie profound !

But death resumed the solemn lyre,
And rous'd afresh the musing choir.

CONSUMPTION next essayed to try :—
Unearthly beam'd her lustrous eye ;
Her cheek had lost its rosy hue ;
Yet she could scarce believe it true.
Her form was cast in beauty's mould,
But her fair limbs looked chilly cold ;
Her brow was wreath'd with lilies fair,
For Lassitude had bound them there,
And twin'd them thickly round her auburn hair.

The harp her gentle fingers tried,
Its tones unloos'd her magic tongue ;
She lean'd her hand against her side,
   And shiver'd as she sung :—

She chose a new and varied lay,
Sometimes tender, sometimes gay—
Languid now and slow, her measures
   Soft, a melancholy strain—
Now her full song repeating Hope's gay pleasures,
Banish'd awhile her sense of present pain.
But ah, although the fascinating theme
Induc'd her soul, of health and joys to dream !
While yet her fingers touch'd each trembling string,
And flattering Hope impell'd the maid to sing—

FEVER advanc'd, and stay'd her hand;—
Deeply she blush'd, and feebly sigh'd,
Then DEATH stretch'd forth his icy wand,
And down she sank, and died!

She died—and Fever's burning hand
Next awoke the sacred lyre;
And as her solemn dirge he sung,
Delirious accents flutter'd on his tongue
And his hot fingers parch'd each sinewy wire!

Next came GOUT, with limping pace,
And show'd the crowd his bloated face;
He nois'd afresh each jocund lay,
Voluptuous song, and roundelay,
With which his halls resounded in his mirthful day.

* * * * * * *

More would have sung, but a joyous shout
Was heard, which put them to the rout;
Drums and hautboys join the sound,
And Mirth was seen light skipping o'er the ground,
With Health, and all her sportive train,
Chasing the phantoms off the plain.

To Poverty.

COLD-HEARTED tyrant, myriads know thy power;
   Myriads, thy captives, feel thy galling chains,
While o'er their heads distressing tempests lower,
And not one golden vision soothes their pains,
Nor e'en one sympathetic spirit deigns
  T" assuage their bitter griefs when thou art by,
Though many a wretch to Affluence complains,
Nor friend nor helper hears their doleful cry,
But all unwept they pine, and unlamented die!

  Pale fiend, companions oft have sever'd been
By thy chill winds, and cordial love withdrawn:
I saw two youthful lovers trip the green,
And each in merry accents hail the morn;
In short they seemèd for each other born,
  And on one pillow wish'd to end their breath;
But by thy arm their prospects all were shorn:
One journey'd on in pleasure's mazy path,
The other, touch'd by thee, soon bow'd to kinder Death!

  Nor age, nor sex has e'er been spar'd by thee:
Thou lay'st the infant on its couch of straw;
Thou robb'st the prattler of its wonted glee,
And mak'st the lively scenes of youth withdraw,
While manhood oft has felt thy painful gnaw,

Blighting his present and his future years;
And Age, e'en venerable Age, I saw
With thee contend, and bath'd in blinding tears,
Sink at th' Oppressor's door, the prey of griefs and fears!

One Winter eve I watch'd thy haggard form,
Shivering, slow limp across the dreary moor,
Thy tatter'd garments sporting in the storm,
When straight thou spied a lonely cottage door—
A cot I ween I oft have seen before,
When scented woodbines climbing, graced its walls,
And roses, there an ever-plenteous store,
Smiling, adorn'd its windows; whilst the calls
From laughing infants, told they knew not thy sad thralls.

But now the scene was chang'd;—the rosied stem
Uncultivated hung—despis'd, forgot;
And the gay flowers, the cold had wither'd them,
And wild gloom hover'd o'er that fated spot,
While the sad inmates murmur'd at their lot,
And laugh'd in anguish at thy demon form,
As gaping fissures in their sad abode,
Received the bitter peltings of the storm,
Which tore the ghastly flame, that burn'd to keep them warm!

This eve, the children cring'd around the hearth,
List'ning in terror to the sounding gale;
While their sad sire sat by in silent wrath,
And the fond mother hush'd her infant's wail;
When from the forest glade thou did'st not fail
To bring them scanty fuel,—two rough brands

I saw them from thee take, when all did hail
The welcome load, as thy enwrinkled hands
Soon made the hearth to glow at their intense commands.

Awhile it burn'd; awhile their sorrow fled,
And some old story crowned the winter scene;—
The children listened with accustomed dread,
And heard of spectres gliding o'er the green,
Or of some shadowy ghost that oft was seen
To haunt the old gray tower in robes of white,
T'avenge their fates who there had murdered been,
Or toll the death-bell to the darksome night—
When hark!—the faggot's crash broke in with dire affright!

Then 'mid the gloom, gaunt Famine glided by,
And through the broken casement mop'd and jeer'd,
His hollow jaws working in mockery
Of mastication, as on all he leer'd:
I saw him give the sign with finger weird
To thee the door to unbar, which straightway done,
In stalk'd the meagre wretch with visage blear'd,
Whose gorgon looks transform'd the group to stone—
Mother, and sire, and babes, and inmates—everyone.

Since then, I've seen thee spoil the village joys:
Its May-day festivals no more are seen;
No more the lawn resounds with sprightly noise
Of rural bands to deck their vernal queen,
Or dance in raptures on the smiling green,
Merry and careless. Now along the air
No beauteous garlands wave, but thy sad mien

The mournful maiden sees, and full of care
Droops like a lily pale, and dies in thy fell snare.

And ah, distressing wretch! thy pangs are known
To those whom heavenly genius fondly charms,
Though their sublimer souls will scarcely own
Thine influence, and laugh at thine alarms;
Yet e'en while some blest Muse their bosom warms
To sing of blissful realms where all is peace,
And tell of lands remote from want or harms,
Thou prey'st on them, nor giv'st them one release,
Till Death convey them home and all their sorrows cease.

I saw the grave of Genius: no tall stone—
No proud memorial—mark'd departed worth;
But there the weary sufferer slept unknown,
And lowly daisies crown'd that spot of earth,
While many a scented violet sprang forth,
And shed a passing fragrance o'er his tomb—
Emblems of him whose ashes rest beneath,
Who's found the goal where sorrows never come,
Far from this vale of tears, in his eternal home!

The People and Jupiter.

(A FABLE).

ON days of yore (no matter when),
   A nation did to Jove complain;
With tears and cries their suit they press'd,
Begging he'd grant them one request.
Jove heard their prayer, and straight descended,
By all the meaner gods attended,
And high amid th' assembled throng,
His cloudy state in ether hung!
Th' astonish'd crowd beneath him bend,
And prayers with adorations blend:
"Great Jove"—they cry—"vouchsafe thine ear,
"And grant to us our fervent prayer—
"Us, destitute, and weak, and small;
"To thee we pray, to thee we call;—
"The meaner creatures of thy sway,
"More agile seem than man, more gay—
"Endow'd with powers of motion far
"Beyond what we thy fav'rites are.
"The lion ranges through the wood,
"The fish divides the watery flood,
"And more, to fowl, the boon is given
"To fly amid th' expanse of heaven:—
"This then our suit—for wings to fly
"Like birds along the azure sky,

"Then heaven shall echo with thy praise,
"And man shall join the warbling lays."
"'Tis done!" said Jove, and shook his mace,
And metamorphised all the race.
Their growing pinions now they try,
And skim along the yielding sky,
Exult in his new favour given,
And 'tend their God half way to heaven!
Now for a season, all is gay;
The people, who so blest as they;
Awhile they skim the boundless air,
And joy and satisfaction share;
'Till by degrees complaints arise,
Harsh frowns, and mutual jealousies.
The lords, the mighty of the state,
Enjoy their pinions all elate,
Till, quite provoking, sure they spy,
With swifter speed the beggar fly;
The poor like eagles flew, the barons
Mov'd slowly on, like limping carrions;
Till quite chagrin'd, they call'd a court,
And at it, all attendance sought;—
Decreed, so sad the state of things,
To tax the poor, and clip their wings!
In vain *they* urge the gift's from Jove;
The nobles know no power above;—
" Ye are our slaves, they frowning cry;
" Submit, or else prepare to die!"
Each answer'd with a dolorous groan,
And sigh'd as clipping day came on;
'Till 'mid the discontented brood
The angry Jove alighting stood:

"Vain man," he thunder'd, "what's not thine
Give up, nor ever more repine;
The gods were mindful of your good,
Before the hills and mountains stood,
But ye our noble gifts despise,
And fondly sue for miseries;
Ye had your boon and no denial;
Ye read your sufferings in the trial.
Know then, to heal your doleful plight,
I take from man the power of flight;—
First, from the poor their wings I take,
That they should no confusion make,
And know ye rich, your limbs are stript,
For clipping others ye are clipt!"

The Beautiful.

(Composed in the Author's 18th year; being the first piece of verse attempted by him.)

SAY what is beautiful? The rural scene,
    When hills and dales are rob'd in smiling green;
When blooming trees their various blossoms show,
And limpid waters in sweet murmurs flow;
When airy songsters in harmonious lays,
Ring heaven's high vault with their Creator's praise;
When marching through the skies, the god of day
Cheers the creation with his 'livening ray.

THE BEAUTIFUL.

Say what is beautiful? When evening shades
Spread their dim curtain o'er the silent glades;
And the ambrosial zeyphyrs as they sweep,
Kiss the dark slumb'ring waters of the deep,
While on its glassy face, the orb of night
Is seen reflected, rob'd in silvery light;
'Tis sweet to watch it dancing on the sea,
Till lost in waves, or dash'd with billowy spray.

Say what is beautiful? The moon to trace,
When wandering in the ample field of space,
With softest radiance tinging cloud on cloud,
Till they, by winds impell'd, her glory shroud;
But from the veil she breaks; a sudden gleam
Here shows the tow'r, and there the gilded stream
And time-worn castle, in whose gloomy cells,
Resounding echo reigns, 'mid num'rous magic spells.

Say what is beautiful? The placid smile
Which on the infant plays;—unknown to toil,
Or life's dire ills, those cherub smiles express
The genuine stamp of peace and happiness—
As the young billows dance upon the sea,
Nor know what hurricanes or tempests be,
But, borne by zephyrs from the gentle west,
They laugh and play, then peaceful sink to rest.

Say what is beautiful? Th' enchanting sound
Of music, waving on the air around,
Which, on the wings of silence, steals its way
To the harmonious realms of purer day:
Again it echos in the groves and woods;
Again reverb'rates on the shining floods;

Then steals its course along the gentle rill
And softly dies while climbing yonder hill.

Say what is beautiful? The pleasing thought
That soon this earth from Ign'rance shall be brought,
And set to glow in Wisdom's mental ray,
And the long night of darkness turn to day;
Then shall men plant the oak and see it rise,
Flourish, and wither, with their lasting eyes,
And 'neath its boughs shall sing Jehovah's praise,
Whilst rocks and sounding vales re-echo with their lays.

The Standard of Truth.

(WRITTEN IN 1832.)

THE Standard of Truth was erected on high;
Its base was the earth, and its summit the sky,
And all tribes gathered near it, with banners unfurl'd,
Summon'd forth by His mandate, who governs the world.

For this standard possesses omnipotent might,
The despot to crush, and the proud to affright;
Though its influence benign makes the earth to revive,
No tyrant can look on its splendour and live!

And there rallied around it, with triumph and songs,
All nations, and languages, peoples and tongues:
The light-hearted children of Freedom were there,
And the blood-stained oppressor was forced to appear;

And the slave and his master; the people and priest;
The learned and rude, from the west to the east—
All came, and attentive was fixed ev'ry eye,
For this test every action and motive could try.

And the trumpet of Liberty sounded a blast,
As before the bright standard the multitude pass'd;
And Oppression and Tyranny heard their own knell,
And look'd on its glory, and stagger'd and fell!

Then there pass'd by the Afric, with slavery's chain,
But the power of that standard soon snapp'd it in twain,
And the darkness of Death which had blinded his eyes,
Was exchang'd for the radiance and light of the skies.

And I mark'd the grim despot of Russia steal by;
Then the Polander girded his sword on his thigh,
And the shouts of the nations in echoes did roll,
As the Autocrat bow'd 'neath the conquering Pole.

Then the Mussulman came, with the Pagan uncouth,
And embrac'd with devotion the Standard of Truth;
And the nations of Europe were gathering there,
And among them Britannia stood proudly and fair:

With joy she beheld her abuses had fled,
And reason and justice replaced in their stead;—
No knave sacrilegiously plunder'd her now,
And the blood of the injured was wip'd from her brow!

And sycophants base from her bosom were thrust,
And merit was rais'd from its dwelling of dust;
And she joined in this chorus, which swell'd to the skies—
"Shout, shout, ye glad nations, lo, tyranny dies!"

The World of Rest.

"There is a calm for those that weep."—J. Montgomery.

WHEN storms of keen anguish o'erwhelm the sad
    And billows of trouble incessantly roll, [soul,
  Or care rages high in the breast,
How consoling's the thought that beyond the blue skies,
Where no tempests e'er ruffle, or dangers arise,
  There's a world of perpetual rest!

Serene is the moon, when in splendour she smiles
O'er the mouldering turrets, or emerald isles,
  That repose on the breast of the deep;
Then the sorrows of life seem all banish'd away,
Or sooth'd into peace 'neath her silvery ray,
  That locks all around into sleep.

Enchanting's the calm when the tempest is o'er, [roar
When the hurricane's sound and the thunder's loud
  Have died in the gentler gale;—
Then we feel some bright gleams of the sunshine of joy,
And our sorrows appear with the tempest to die,
  And visions of pleasure we hail.

But more calm is the scene in those regions of light;—
There, streams in eternal tranquility glide,
  And flow'rets perennial bloom;
And there far removed from distresses or woes,
The weary enjoy everlasting repose,
  And find it a heavenly home!

On Seeing a Daisy Growing in November.

I SAW the daisy rise,
 A solitary flower,
It might have bloomed 'neath fairer skies,
 Or deck'd some rural bow'r;
Or help'd to stud the smiling plain,
Water'd by April's balmy rain.

 But cruel Fate decreed,
 A birth-place for it here,
To catch the gale, which o'er the mead
 Sighs to the aged year;
And plac'd it near a brooklet's side
That now forsaken, rolls its tide!

 Soon must its beauties die,
 For angry temptests low'r;
Winter, with hoary frosts is nigh,
 To blast the lovely flow'r;
And beating rains will lay its head
Neglected, on the earth's cold bed!

 Relic of other days!
 Sweet Spring's delightful pride!
Could I but bear thee 'neath its rays,
 I should be overjoyed;
For ah! thou wing'st my Fancy home,
Where storms and tempests never come!

On thee I'd drop a tear,
    And as it o'er thee flows,
Pity would sigh for those that bear
    Adversity's sad woes;
For, beauteous flower! like thee I've seen
Numbers who bend 'neath sorrows keen.

I've seen the youthful bard,
    Warm with poetic fire,
Undaunted, strike an angel's chord,
    And tune a seraph's lyre,
In strains so lofty and sublime,
That they defy the hand of Time.

But in a dreary cot
    The poet pin'd alone;
Nor was there (such his painful lot)
    A friend to sooth his moan;—
The clouds of woe did o'er him swell—
Unpitied and unwept he fell!

And thou, sweet flow'r, must die;—
    And when thy form is fled,
Many like thee—no helper nigh—
    Will sink among the dead;
But Hope still points beyond the tomb,
Where amaranths perennial bloom!

Christmas.

NOW Christmas, jolly Christmas,
    Is come our hearts to cheer;
With holly crown'd, and misletoe,
    The monarch of the year.
With merry din invite him in,
    And heap the yule-logs higher;
And pour the wine, that all may join
    To greet the good old sire!

For hark! the gale is rising,
    The winds blow loud and strong;
And, on the gloomy storm-cloud thron'd,
    Dark winter sweeps along!
But what care we? With mirth and glee,
    While Beauty's eye shines bright,
Blithe hours we'll spend, and our old friend
    Shall be our guest to-night.

O! Christmas, social Christmas,
    In cottage and in hall,
To old and young a welcome friend,
    Alike belov'd of all;
To hear thy voice, our babes rejoice,
    And clap their tiny hands;
While age with thee can jocund be,
    And join the festive bands.

With game, and dance, and carol,
    We'll hail thee as of yore;
To thee, from many a flowing bowl,
    A rich libation pour.
And while the snow in drifts doth blow,
    While moans the dreary blast,
Our mirth and joys shall higher rise,
    Away our cares we'll cast.

O! Christmas, sacred Christmas,
    From yonder village bells,
To herald thy majestic step,
    The pealing music swells;
And voices rise 'neath midnight skies,
    In holy solemn strain,
To tell how He of Bethlehem,
    Was born on earth to reign!

Come, come with ancient Christmas,
    To yonder hallow'd pile,
And hear the sounding anthem roll,
    Along the lengthened aisle:
With footsteps slow, up let us go
    Where our forefathers trod,
To linger there in fervent prayer,
    And hear the man of God!

O! Christmas, fleeting Christmas,
    Thou ever journey'st on,
Though memory dwells o'er vanish'd hopes,
    And lov'd ones dead and gone.
Thou may'st not stay, but far away,
    Through Winter's dreary halls,

To meet the year, thou dost appear,
   The bright new year that calls!

And onward, ever onward,
   Through realms of frost and snow,
'Till winter merges into spring,
   And wild March trumpets blow.
Soon will the day, with length'ning ray,
   Foretel the summer flowers;—
But now they're here, with mirth and cheer,
   We'll keep the Christmas hours.

Thoughts in Spring.

THERE is a sadness in the Spring
   Amidst its glorious blossoming;
Though flowers their dazzling forms unfold,
And rainbows span the skies of gold;
Though Earth, wak'd up from the winter's sod
With her hundred voices tells of God;—
Though the child may play through the merry May,
And welcome Nature's holiday;—
Though the birds may sing to the jocund Spring,
While with their glad notes the vallies ring,
To me these scenes sad recollections bring.

I have felt their power in the noontide hour,
When the fitful wind shook tree and flower;—
It seem'd to say "Ah wherefore gay?
"Thy early friends are far away,

"With them thou'st pluck'd Spring's fragrant bloom,
"But flowers now blossom round their tomb."
Yon oak still lives, that gnarlèd thing,
Young leaves from its old branches spring,
Like Hopes awak'ning from Despair;
Th' repose of centuries is there!
There's a voice in the tree;—it speaks to me—
"Where are the youths that sported with thee,
"And the maidens that sang enchantingly?
"I have spread out my boughs for their cool retreat"—
Alas, old Oak they are dead at thy feet!

A butterfly pass'd, with its robe of light,
Cheating my fancy, and mocking my sight;—
'Tis hid in a flower,—now here, now there,
Like a vision that floats on the dreamy air;—
Gay phantom of childhood, where Memory clings,
Thou bearest the Past on thy beautiful wings—
I am roaming again where I sported of yore,
And behold the fair scenes of my childhood once more!

  I stood beside a crystal spring,
  Whose waters, ever murmuring,
  Creep 'neath the tangled grass and spread
  Cool streams along their pebbly bed.
  I love to track this streamlet wild;
  It was my mirror when a child,
  And every changeful year I look
  Upon this little faithful brook,
  Whose waters roll as fresh and fair,
  As when a boy I wandered there.
  But childhood and its dreams are faded;
  Years of care my brow have shaded;

Hopes which came on golden wings,
Have passed, and only left their stings,
While Memory with her busy train
Evokes those years of Hope again!
Thus sorrows lurk in Spring's bright hours,
As snakes oft hide 'neath fairest flowers;
And yet 'twere hard indeed to say
If we should wish them quite away,
Or why these scenes, so fair to view,
Should not afford instruction too.

The Orphan's Dream.

THE flow'rets closed their cups of gold,
    As the curfew was sounding afar,
As the gurgling waters serenely roll'd,
    Beneath the evening star;

And the moon's fair orb illumin'd the sky,
    As it sprang from the dark-blue wave,
When a lonely orphan stole silently,
    To watch o'er her parents' grave.

The bat flittered by, as with mournful step
    She pac'd the path that she oft had trod;
But she found the place where her parents slept,
    And sank on the dewy sod.

The dewy sod she made her bed,
    And her sorrowful tears fell thickly around,

Whilst the dim mist arose and curtain'd her head,
   As it lay on the new-risen mound.

Sad pillow for such a helpless one!
   Yet no kind supporter was nigh,
Her woes to condole, or hush her sad moan,
   Or close the orphan's eye.

The winds pip'd loud, and the cypress shook,
   And the woods caught the owlet's moan,
Which rous'd the pale phantoms from every nook,
   To flitter around the tall stone.

But the orphan cared not for owlet's song,
   Nor the ghostly spectres of night,
Nor the cold grey mist that brought along
   The shadowy forms of affright.

But she call'd to her parents:—"Oh, let me in,
   "To rest in your dark and silent abode,
"Where the wicked no longer tempt to sin,
   "Nor sorrows more corrode!"

She call'd, and the phantoms answer'd her voice,
   And wav'd their gaunt hands in the air,
And beckon'd each other to haste to her cries,
   And throng to the orphan there.

They supported her head, and sooth'd her soul,
   And around her their watch did keep,
Whilst she bended beneath their dreamy control,
   And sunk in the arms of sleep.

A holy dream then possess'd her mind:—
   She thought there appear'd to her sight,

THE ORPHAN'S DREAM.

Her parents supported by angel-kind,
   And array'd in robes of white.

About her head they hover'd long,
   While their splendour eclips'd the fair moon;
And they chanted aloud a glorious song,
   Of the land of perpetual noon.

Then her pallid cheek they fondly press'd,
   And whisper'd, "Sleep on, my child,
"And dream of the realms of endless rest,
   "Beyond these regions wild.

"In the earth's cold bosom our forms of clay,
   "Are taking their last long sleep,
"But our spirits rejoice in endless day,
   "And around thee their vigils keep.

"Then grieve not, dear child, for thy parents fled,
   "Let tears not bedew thy face,
"For thou too shalt rest among the still dead,
   "And fly to our embrace!"

The orphan dream'd on, and saw them arise,
   Borne aloft by etherial air,
And saw them await at the gates of the skies,
   And mix with the shining ones there.

The midnight bell toll'd—the orphan wak'd, [light
   And walk'd to her home 'neath the moon's pallid
But her sorrowful heart no longer ached,
   When she thought on her dream that night.

Birthday Verses.

TO AN ONLY DAUGHTER.

ANNE, dear object of my love,
   My solace and my care,
For thee to bounteous heaven above,
   I breathe a fervent prayer:
Great Parent hear me whilst I pray,
For blessings on her natal day!

Not the proud glittering pomp of state
   That riches might bestow,
Nor all the honours that await
   The great ones as they go,
Nor beauty's captivating power,
Thy father covets for thy dower.

But oh! may peace thy steps attend—
   That peace which heaven bestows;
And high imperial virtue lend
   Her influence till life's close;
And sweet content with modest grace
Beam radiant from thy youthful face!

My only daughter, dearest tie,
   That binds my roving heart,
Thy form I view with fancy's eye,
   As days and years depart,
With fairy step and spirits light
Bounding before my raptured sight!

Or walking by the streamlet's side,
   With meditative mien,—
Where I before have oft espied
   Great Nature's bounteous scene,—
Entranc'd with wonder, love, and joy,
As her deep myst'ries meet thine eye.

Anne, should length of days be given,
   This vision may prove true;
But if a babe, thou'rt call'd to heav'n,
   A fairer scene to view,
Oh, may thy parents bear the stroke,
Nor wish heav'n's mandate to revoke!

Then little prattler get thee forth,
   Upon life's fleeting tide,
The world before thee with its worth,
   And Providence thy guide;
And when this dream of life is past,
May heav'n receive thy soul at last!

A Winter Piece.

THE wintry day had clos'd, and the pale moon,
   Full orb'd and clear, had risen o'er the hills,
And usher'd in the eve of Christmas, as
A lonely orphan boy was plodding slow
His weary way without a friend or home.
It was a bitter pang that rent his breast,

As he looked in at the bright blazing fires
That gilded many a social hearth, and heard
The shouts and glee of happy inmates there,
For he was desolate;—no home had he,
Kindred or friends, to greet him with a smile,
Or voice to wisper comfort to his soul!
A-cold he was, yet nought but tatter'd clothes
Had he to cover him, which the wind shook,
As it blew fitfully, and forced a tear
From out his sunken eyes, which fell and froze
An icy pearl, as cold as his sad heart.
Onward he went, and left the busy town;
He could not bear to hear its merry bells
Resounding through the night, so hurried on;
They seem'd to mock his soul, for so of old
They chim'd, when he, a happy school-boy, laugh'd
As gay as any at this festive hour.
But now his parents rested in their graves,
O'er which the snow had spread a chilly sheet,
And he was left a wanderer o'er the world.
Yet had he honest pride, that scorn'd to beg,
So took his matches (penury's sad ware),
And sold them as he pass'd from door to door.

Ye hearts that now enjoy a Christmas feast,
While snugly seated round the social hearth,
Think, as ye hear the bitter biting wind
Without the casement—think, and feel for those
Who share in no such festivals as these,
But listen to them, and sighing pass our streets!

For a Sunday School Anniversary.

Composed by request, and publicly recited by one of the Scholars.

YE friends of children, an assembled throng,
    Attend the lispings of an infant's tongue;
Accept the humble gratitude we pay,
To you, who bent our steps in Wisdom's way—
Who taught us folly's downward path to shun,
And bow our knees before th' eternal throne—
Who led our feet to Salem's blest abode,
And taught our infant lips to whisper "God."
But for your care, we still had sin pursued,
And deep in dreadful guilt our souls imbrued;
Perhaps had never learn'd the way to heaven,
Or how to have our num'rous sins forgiven;—
Had never learn'd God's holy name to fear,
His Word to read, his Sabbaths to revere;—
Had never learned the truths that Jesus died
Our souls to save, and lives to be our guide;
Nor e'er had known to breathe a simple prayer
To Him who makes a little child His care;
Who, while on earth, to babes vouchsaf'd His love,
And said "Of such my kingdom is above;"
Who, while sweet meekness beam'd around His face,
Took in His tender arms our helpless race,
Clasp'd them with love and pity to His breast,
And with His sov'reign voice pronounced us "blest."

Kind was his thought, benevolent his plan,
Who first to form a Sabbath School began;
Who saw the peasant youth neglected lie,
And like the good Samaritan pass'd by,
Reclaim'd them from their ignorance and vice,
And train'd his lowly pupils for the skies.
What different scenes our Sabbaths now present
To those 'ere youth at first to School were sent!
No loit'ring bands in careless groups are seen,
Or idly wand'ring o'er the village green;
Or, cloth'd in rags, wear out the sacred day
In wanton mischief, or in noisy play—
Their vacant minds on sin and folly bent,
And thankful when the tedious hours were spent;—
But now, when morn awakes the happy day,
Blithe as a lark, we shake dull sleep away,
Pay our orisons to our maker God,
Then straight pursue the path we oft have trod.
How blest the scene! how admirably sweet,
When all our little band together meet!
When with united voice a hymn of praise,
Before our heav'nly Father's throne we raise;
When with our teachers at His feet, we bend,
And simple prayers with adorations blend,
Or in the various duties of the hours,
We strive to emulate each other's powers,
'Till at the close, again we join in praise,
And end as we begin our holy days.
Blest exercises, who their worth can speak!
To tell their good, our tongues are far too weak;
The theme demands an angel's noblest strain,
The mighty blessings fully to explain!

For this blest cause, kind friends, we now implore
You to contribute of your earthly store;
The deed will please the Power that sits on high,
And feeds the hungry ravens when they cry;
And when, reclining on the bed of death,
You to your Maker offer up your breath,
It shall be ours to prop your aged head,
And round your couch our earnest prayers to shed;
And with soft gratitude to close your eyes,
While angels waft your spirits to the skies;
And should we meet upon heav'n's blissful shore—
Our sorrows ended, and our troubles o'er—
Your love to us we will again review,
Together shout in strains for ever new,
And join in nobler praise to whom all praise is due!

Inscription for a Cemetery.

STAY, reader, pause upon this peaceful spot;
There is a peace, the worldling knoweth not—
Profound as silence in the stillest night,
Yet, as the glorious summer noontide, bright;—
'Tis as the concord of melodious sounds,
And lifts the soul beyond earth's narrow bounds,
It gives a presage of the joys to come—
Reveals fair glimpses of th' eternal home;
'Tis harmony with God, and things divine;
It "passeth understanding;" make it thine.

The Prisoner of Eld.

I remember reading many years back, a story of some one who for an offence committed in his early days, was condemned to labor in a prison for the term of a hundred years. The narrative stated that he lived to complete the period, and then left his dungeon; but finding the friends of his youth all dead, and feeling lonely and disconsolate, he begged to be re-admitted. His prayer was granted. He was received again within its gloomy walls, but had scarce crossed the threshold, when he staggered and fell down dead. Deeming this subject a proper one for a short poem, I have tried my hand upon it.

"THY task is over, thy work is done;
 "Old man, thou again art free;—
"Well hast thou borne thy toil, lone one,
 "Thou hast pass'd thy century,
"So prithee take thy hat and begone,
 "And enjoy thy liberty!

"The sun is tinging the bright green hills,
 "As erst in the days of yore,
"And there's music as sweet in the murmuring rills,
 "As ever was heard before;
"And the butterfly's drest in as gay a robe
 "As any she ever wore.

"And hearts, young hearts, are beating still
 "With hope, and love, and joy,
"And now as ever, their bosoms thrill
 "With the bounding ecstacy;—
"Come re-unite with the happy throng
 "And join in their mirth and glee."

THE PRISONER OF ELD.

"Oh, do not mock me!" the old man cried,
    And turn'd from the sight away;
Then with slow tott'ring footsteps hied
    To the place where his lost ones lay,
Within the graveyard's hallowed ground;
    But their very tombs were gray!

And the ruthless hand of Time had defaced
    The names that each headstone bore;—
With eye and finger the old man traced
    Those chisel'd lines of yore;
But all in vain—his aching sight
    Could not the names explore.

The sexton proffer'd his aid to lend,
    (An ancient man was he),
"Whoe'er thou seekest, my hoary friend,
    "Must surely be known to me,
"For I've delv'd here with mattock and spade,
    "Full sixty years and three."

The stranger's tears fell thick and fast,
    As with faltering voice and low,
A gentle name from his lips there pass'd—
    A name of the long ago;—
The puzzled sexton look'd aghast,
    For the name he did not know.

Then the wanderer left the dead, and sped
    To the little town hard by;
Its streets he pac'd with silent tread,
    And disappointed eye,
For nothing there could he recognize
    Of ought beneath the sky.

Chang'd, chang'd!—the cot where he dwelt lang syne,
    Was swept from the place away,
And in its stead a mansion fine
    Rose stately, and proud, and gay;
So strange its grandeur seem'd, he turn'd
    With averted face away!

Lonely he stood in the busy street,
    Like a wreck on some barren strand;
No well-known voice did a welcome greet,
    No comrade clasp'd his hand;—
He stood, a solitary thing,
    In his old fatherland.

Then he turn'd his steps to the dungeon grim,
    From whence he of late had stray'd;
Its clanking chains were music to him;
    Of the warders he friends had made;
And again to enter its gloomy walls,
    With fervour the old man pray'd.

His suit was granted; he moved to his cell,
    And upon him was bolted the door,
But scarce had he enter'd, when lo! he fell
    A corpse on the prison floor!
"Old man thy toils are all ended now,
    "And nothing shall grieve thee more!"

Wellington:

OBIT, SEPTEMBER, 1852.*

OH, mourn for the Hero of heros departed!
    Lament, for Britannia's fam'd chief is no more!
He is gone, the brave patriot, the just, the true-hearted;
His counsels are ended, his conflicts are o'er!

Like a calm golden sunset, in peace and in glory,
Sublimely he sinks in his time-honour'd tomb,
And ages to ages shall echo the story,
How Europe he rescued from rapine and doom.

When the daring Usurper caus'd monarchs to tremble,
And panic-struck nations grew pale with affright,
The thunder of Jove did his prowess resemble,
And Waterloo tells of great Wellington's might.

Nor Europe alone had his arm to protect her;
Hindostan's swarthy empire his courage maintain'd;
And the millions there rul'd by Britannia's mild sceptre
The conquerer thank for high victories gain'd.

Nor only for conquests renown'd shall we praise him;
The olive with laurel shall twine round his bier;
For his counsels and deeds in the senate shall raise him,
Among the Immortals whoses name we revere.

With Duty his watchword, his course ever loyal
To God and his sov'reign, his country he serv'd,

---

* The two first and the two last stanzas of this elegy have been set to music.

And safely through anarchy, danger, and trial,
Our altars, our homes, and our freedom preserv'd.

Peace, peace to his manes! with princes in quiet,
With bards and with senators fam'd let him lie;
O, death! o'er his ashes alone can'st thou riot—
Enshrin'd in our hearts his *worth* never can die!

Sonnet,

Composed at sunrise, September 30th, 1857—(A remarkably red morning). Intelligence of the cruelties inflicted upon the English by *Nana Sahib* and other conspirators, concerned in the Indian mutiny, had just been received, causing a general shudder throughout Britain.

THE crimson curtains of aurorian cloud
   Are spread o'er land and sea with angry flush,
As if the sun with very shame doth blush
And hide himself within a gory shroud
At sight of scenes forbidden;—wailings loud;
Women in agony, and slaughter'd babes;
The young and fair sent to untimely graves,
By cruel lust and lawless rapine bow'd!
Lo, now he bears to occidental lands
The blood-red ensign of the wrath of Ind;—
Upon the clouds I see the tort'ring fiend,
And murder'd shapes before my vision swell!
Yet while I gaze, they change to cherub bands,
And saint-like forms, mid' fields of asphodel!

Sonnet.

IF on the lonely ear at eventide,
   Strange symphonies in witching cadence fell
From the blue heavens—now with a sudden swell,
Now soft as angel's whisper on the void—
How should we pause and list'n! the ear o'erjoy'd,
Would task the mind to tell what powers unseen
Scatter'd the far-off music; had it been
Hymning from age to age on every side,
'Twould furnish proof convincing, eloquent,
Of seraph regions and celestial quires
Touching perpetually their golden wires,
To tell of heaven and joys that never die:—
Yet to the sister sense, no less are sent
From stars, high hints of immortality.

Honour.

HONOUR'S a shade that flies if you pursue it—
   A butterfly that quits you if you'd view it;
But leave ambition unconcern'd, when lo!
The shadow follows you where'er you go;
Descend the steep of pride, with wings outspread,
The butterfly alights upon your head,
And those who wait at honour's sacred shrine
Twine blooming wreaths and consecrate them thine.

Sonnet,

To MR. J. W. DALBY, author of many beautiful poems which have appeared from time to time in the "Northampton Mercury," and other periodicals. Like Burns, "J. W. D." is an Exciseman, and therefore often has to change his place of abode. I spent a very pleasant evening with him at Duston some years back, but he has left that village, and I know not where he is now located.

PERIPATETIC poet, wandering bard,
    Whose song from many a sylvan nook and dell,
Like note of thrush erst on mine ears did swell;
Or like the lark, that rises from the sward
To heav'n's high gates, and as he mounting, sings,
And shakes the dew-drops from his rising wings,
So didst thou sparkle in thy healthful lay.
Where dost thou nestle, now that spring is come?
Is Buckingham's old rural town thy home?
Does classic Olney tempt thee there to stray?
Where'er thou art, thou lovest Nature's charms,
And hast the power her beauties to rehearse;
Then sing anew, while Spring thy bosom warms,
    For gentle scenes should live in gentle verse.

May, 1858.

Song.

MY true love is gone to his rest;
   He has lain himself down in the tomb,
Where the night winds roll over his breast,
   And sweet-scented violets bloom.

The cold turf is wrapping his clay;—
   Flow'rets spring where his corpse is asleep;
O'er his grave will I bend all the day,
   And there all the night will I weep.

Then pity a maiden forlorn,
   Whose heart is distracted with care;
Whose bosom with anguish is torn;
   Whose frame is the prey of despair!

Oh, his eye was as bright as the star
   That flames on the forehead of heaven,
And his countenance lovely and fair,
   As any that nature has given!

But that eye now in darkness is seal'd;
   The earthworm has made him its prey;—
To his grave by the moonlight I'll steal,
   And there will I weep all the day.

Then pity a maiden forlorn,
   Whose heart is distracted with care;
Whose bosom with anguish is torn;
   Whose frame is the prey of despair!

The Heart-stricken:

A BALLAD.

"She never told her love,
"But let concealment like a worm i' the bud
"Feed on her damask cheek."
SHAKSPEARE.

ACROSS the green at close of day,
   Stole forth a maiden fair;
Her blushing cheeks look'd beautiful,
   And loosely flow'd her hair.

Full hastily she pass'd along,
   Nor guess'd a mortal knew
What passion heav'd her bosom fair,
   Or gave her cheek its hue.

Still on she went, and as she went,
   From her fair eye so blue,
There fell a bright, a crystal tear,
   And mingled with the dew:

It mingled with the pearly dew,
   Which to the sun is given,
To form a rainbow in the skies,
   And shine afresh in heaven.

Still on she went—no sound was heard
   Of footstep far or near;—
"Why stays he?" deeply sigh'd the maid;
   "My Henry should be here."

THE HEART-STRICKEN.

The skies hung out their golden lamps,
    The dews fell thick around,
The hour-bell toll'd, and the night wind roll'd,
    But the maiden kept her ground.

Who lov'd like her? who felt like her?
    As echo caught his voice,
"My Henry comes," she smiling said,
    "And I shall be his choice!"

But while the smile was on her face—
    That face so wonderous fair—
And words were on her gentle tongue,
    She found another there:

Another girl had won his heart,
    And hung upon his arm,
And shar'd the false one's falsest smiles,
    And felt his kisses warm!

The maiden sigh'd afresh, and left
    The rending, hateful sight;
But her heart beat cold with love despised,
    And the damps which fell that night.

And a shivering seiz'd her gentle frame,
    And her health forsook her cheek,
But she no one told why her heart beat cold,
    Though that heart was like to break.

She meekly bore her heavy woes,
    By her false love belied,
'Till, like a fair but smitten flower,
    She pined away and died!

The Forsaken Maid.

A TYPOGRAPHICAL EPISTLE TO A FRIEND.

DEAR Friend, I take my pen in ☞,
   But write with heavy heart,
Hoping to make you understand
   The secrets I impart.

For not to all would I reveal
   My wrongs and miseries;
Therefore by *points* my griefs conceal,
   And use ' s.

My trembling quill I scarce ‚nd,
   My sorrows are so great;
Nor can Time's renovating hand
   Heal my afflicted state.

My hopes are —— d, my lover's fled,
   The pole * of my life
Has woo'd another in my stead,
   And took her for a wife.

The direful tidings pierced me through,
   Like † s in my breast;
Like ‡ s strike anew,
   And rob my soul of rest.

The .'s past of tranquil joys
   And dreams of fancied bliss,
Clos'd from the world and all its noise
   In Love's ( ).

THE FORSAKEN MAID.

My bosom like a : fire
   From Cupid's alter burn'd,
For him, my lord, my heart's desire,
   Who now my love has spurn'd.

O, how I longed his face to view,
   How prized his salutation ;
And thought each tender *billet-doux*
   A !

His " ever charm'd my ear,
   So musical they fell ;
In form and worth did none appear
   My lover's ‖.

But he is false, and I'm undone ;
   Ah, miserable day !
Each § of my life must run
   In sad complaints away.

I ? if I long can bear
   My weight of heavy sorrow ;
To-day the victim of despair,
   The same sad wretch to-morrow.

Pity my woes, my dearest friend,
   Beyond all computations ;
So now my ¶ I end
   In bitter ! ! ! !

Arcadia.

A PASTORAL.

I HAVE been in Arcady;
 Pleasant scenes have met mine e'e,
Known in realms of Poesy;
And as I wandered o'er the plains,
I hail'd them in these simple strains:—
" Gentle zephyr! blow and rock me;
" Sportive echo! wake and mock me;
" For upon the blooming bed
" Which Flora for Narcissus spread,
" I would lie, and see the day
" Roll with bubb'ling streams away.
" Sweetness smiles on every side;
" Brooks by swelling hillocks, glide—
" Swelling hillocks, which resound
" With the rustic tabor's sound;
" Pipes and past'ral reeds I hear,
" Waking echo everywhere.
" Up the sloping mountain's steep,
" Youths and maidens slowly creep,
" Follow'd by their fleecy charge,
" Which feed in peace, or roam at large.
" Happy shepherds, who appear
" Undisturb'd by care or fear!
" You, nor toil, nor turmoil know—
" Free from strife and free from woe,
" Free from science' vexing lore,

"Or philosophy's strong power;
"Sweet your songs in concert join,
"Peace and joy around you twine!
"I would watch you, 'till the day
"Dies with western gales, away;
"Then, amid your folds, I'd stray,
"While Cynthia holds her tranquil sway,
"And behold the silent sheep
"On the greensward fast asleep!
"Happy shepherds! peaceful swains!
"For your comfort, nature deigns
"To ope her lap, and spread her store,
"Round your borders, o'er and o'er!"
But yonder walks a youth, with aspect fair,
Whose bounding breast seems light as summer air;
Whose long loose tresses round his forehead flow—
His forehead, white as is the spotless snow;
Forth from his form beam innocence and love;
The gales caress him as around they move:
DAMON his name—the sprightliest of the throng—
His praises flow from every maiden's tongue;
But these no angry jealousy awake,
For no rude noise their love or concord break:
The youths and maidens led him to the bowers,
Where jovial shepherds chant away the hours;
And as young Damon saw the motley throng,
He warbled clear this brief spontaneous song:—
"Youths and maidens, come with me;
"Let us trace the steps of Love;
"Round yon' grassy hillocks, see
"Fairest flowers her presence prove.
"She it is that ever gives

"A zest to all our varied pleasures;
"By her power, Arcadia lives,
"Surrounded by kind Nature's treasures.
"What's the flow'ret, without Love?
"A poor unmeaning gaudy thing.
"Oft have the pink and violet strove,
"Which to her fam'd shrine should bring
"Sweetest odours, richest stores,
"To shed around these healthful shores!
"Love, attended by the Graces,
"Oft our beauteous valley paces;
 With her, the Parnassian Nine,
"On our couches oft recline,
"And hear the streamlet's gentle tide,
"Down the pebbly shelvings glide;
"Or listen to sweet Philomel,
"Softly warbling in the dell.
"Hark! I hear Love's gentle tread,
"Bounding o'er the flow'ry mead,
"Strewing garlands in her way,
"As she skippeth light and gay.
"Youths and maidens with me rove;
"Let us trace the steps of Love!"

Young Damon ended, but his pleasant strains
Long filled the ears of all the list'ning swains,
Who tun'd their pipes afresh with jocund glee,
In cheerful notes, that sounded o'er the lea:
When these were hush'd, young Corydon's soft lay,
In pensive strains thus woo'd the parting day:—

"Youths and Maidens, come with me,
"Let us rouse Simplicity;—

" Neath the shelvèd bank she's sleeping,
" Where the sparkling tide is creeping—
" Mid' the tangled foliage green,
" Where no evil thing is seen.
" Willows o'er her head are weeping;
" Scarce a noontide ray is creeping,
" Through the secret cool recess,
" Where she hides her modest face.
" Let us rouse her gentle form;
" Her calm features know no storm;
" Her's are no scholastic rules—
" Philosophy was made for fools!
" Let the sons of Science show
" Why the bright celestial bow
" That bestrides the sinking cloud,
" Thus should shine in colours proud;—
" Let him say 'tis all deceit—
" All an unsubstantial cheat—
" The glitt'ring pageant of an hour,
" Evanishing amid the shower:
" We would tell how Iris spun it,
" And how bright Apollos won it;—
" We account it made of beryl,
" Gold, and amethyst, and pearl—
" The tall portal of the skies,
" Where unceasing pleasure lies!
" Let him say the light's great fount,
" Which now gilds the western mount,
" Sets—in other realms to fly;
" Sets—to robe another sky:
" We would say the orb has found
" Our fair earth's far-distant bound,

"And as shades the landscape wrap,
"Gently sinks in Thetis' lap;—
"Then, the sparkling stars of night
"Sweetly lend their beauteous light,
"Scatter'd o'er the heavenly blue,
"Shining with a glorious hue!
"Then, fair evening's gentle queen,
"Rises midst the quiet scene,
"Tinging bright the fleecy cloud,
"That her witching influence woo'd;—
"Then the pensive lover steals
"O'er the dewy lawns, and feels
"Tender thoughts within him rise,
"And full oft he stops and sighs;
"Then we shepherds sink in sleep,
"While around us fairies creep,
"And with many a jocund lay,
"Sportive pass the night away.
"Ours is not the pomp and show,
"Fashion's glittering victims know.
"Bounteous nature, grant thy store,
"We would never covet more!
"Youths and maidens come with me;
"Let us rouse Simplicity!

He ceas'd, and now the radiant orb of day
Had sunk, and from the east, the twilight gray
Stole o'er the plain, when gentle sleep oppress'd
The drowsy sense, and soon each flutt'ring breast
Was still'd, for all had sunk in balmy rest.

To ――――

ON THE RECEIPT OF A LOCK OF HAIR.

To add to her beauties, her dark flowing tresses
  In ringlets soft shaded her forehead so fair,
When from —— I requested, with smiles and caresses,
A gift the most tender—a lock of her hair.

She granted the boon with the sweetest good-nature,
And gave me a braid in my bosom to wear;—
I exclaim'd as I took it "I'd part with each treasure
Of earth, ere I'd part with this lov'd lock of hair."

Should the storms of adversity blacken around me,
And bane and misfortune afflict me with care;— [me,
Though an ocean of sorrow should threaten to drown
I'd smile as I gaze on the lock of her hair!

Or should Fortune's bright sun ever gild my horizon,
I'd secure it with gold in a casket most rare;
But gold, or whatever the world sets a price on,
I esteem but as dross to the lock of her hair!

It shall call to my mind all those dear recollections—
So long as I pass through this desert of care—
Of love and the scenes of my early affections;
And I'll sigh as I gaze on the lock of her hair!

And when years have roll'd onward, and Time's chilly finger,
Hath silver'd my forehead, or stript it quite bare,
On the gift then unchang'd, my dim vision shall linger,
And a tear shall let fall on the lock of her hair!

To ——

Yes! thou art beauteous as the summer flowers;
　　Fair as the gentle moon without a shade;
Cheerful as are the birds on verdant bowers;
Sweet as the secret violet, lowly laid!
Thine amber ringlets down thy forehead flow;
Thy cheeks the lily and the rose combine;
Thy bosom's pure, as is the mountain snow;
Thine eyes like glancing stars with beauty shine;
Unto thy voice a music's charm is given;
Thy frown's despair; thy smile alone is heaven!

Stanzas.

The first young dream of early love
　　I e'en remember still;
The pleasing vision charm'd my soul,
　　And so it ever will:

For there was something in that hour
　　So exquisitely wild;—
The sun-light fell with magic power;
　　The landscape sweeter smiled.

The hidden meaning then I knew
　　Of all things rich and rare—
Knew why the rose was beautiful,
　　And why the lily fair.

Each star that beams in heav'n above,
  Each flow'r that blooms below,
Glow'd with a strange, a mystic love
  It thrill'd my heart to know.

And she, dear empress of that heart,
  In innocence array'd,
Who breath'd the soft bewitching spell,
  I Nature's teacher made!

Her eye, the ocean's azure depths
  Reflected fair and clear;
Her teeth were spotless pearls; her cheeks—
  Sweet roses blossom'd there.

Each pleasing form, each beauteous thing,
  Was symbol'd forth in her;
Each did to her its meaning bring—
  She their Interpreter.

O woman, angel-sister, friend!
  To thee alone is given,
The charm to gild the scenes of earth,
  And point beyond to heav'n!

Epigram:

WRITTEN ON THE BACK OF A QUACK DOCTOR'S CIRCULAR.

ALL ye beneath the various ills
  Of sore disease opprest,
Take Dr. W———'s famous pills,
And soon you'll lie at rest.

Epigram:

ON A BAD SINGER.

'TWAS said Cecelia's ever-tuneful voice
    Once charm'd an angel from the radiant skies;
But should our hero in such feats engage,
He'd raise a demon from the other place.

Enigma.

(FOR THE LADIES.)

A BONY monster, gaunt and slim—
    Oft' seen without a head or limb—
I, on the fair securely prey,
And hecatombs of victims slay.
I steal the maiden's rosy hue,
And dim her eyes of heavenly blue;
Distort her form, corrupt her breath,
And leave her to disease and death;—
Insidiously I work her ill,
Yet, strange to say, she loves me still,
And clasps me to her bosom white,
Where oft I lurk conceal'd from sight,
And eat her beauty like the moth;
Yet the poor maiden, nothing loth,
The more she is by me oppress'd,
The closer hugs me to her breast:—

Ladies, if this be truth, endorse it,
Prize health, and throw away your *Corset*.

The Talisman.

THERE is a power, a magic power,
   Surpassing Eastern story,
Without whose aid Apollo's sons
   Can never climb to glory;—
It nerves the arm, it fires the song,
   It aids each bold endeavour,
It bears the ardent soul along,
   Like a resistless river :
And yet, though mighty thus it be,
   It may be found in letters three.

It causes obstacles to yield,
   It prompts to deeds of daring,
It bears the warrior through the field,
   When he'd be else despairing ;
It overcomes opposing strife ;
   It makes the stubborn plastic ;
It kindles bright the lamp of life
   In hearts enthusiastic ;
Its name's an "open sesame"
   To science, lore, and poesy !

Without it, talent is but tame,
   And lightly priz'd the scholar ;—
With it, however high the aim,
   Success is sure to follow.
Fame bears it on her shining brow,
   When gathering crowds admire her,

    And Genius, whether high or low,
        When lofty thoughts inspire her :—
    What is this strong activity ?
        This precious influence ? N R G.

    It bore Columbus on his way
        Across the trackless ocean ;
    Gave Mexico to Cortes' sway ;
        Set Arkwrights' wheels in motion ;—
    And still the force electric lives
        In garret, school, and college,
    To fire each dauntless soul, that strives
        To climb the tree of knowledge :
    Then reader, let your motto be—
        X L C R and N R G !

Lines to Earl Grey:

[Written at the crisis in 1831, just prior to the passing of the Reform Bill.]

HAIL venerable statesman ! patriot, hail !
    Britain rejoices at thy honor'd worth,
And thunders forth her gratitude to thee ;
Enrolls thy name in history, and stamps
The glowing record with eternal fame ;
For thou with firm undaunted aspect, long
Hast borne the lash of scorn and infamy,
And iron-tongued oppression, like the rock
That lifts its awful summit mid' the wars
Of troubled waters, and beats back their waves !

LINES TO EARL GRAY.

Now Britain sees thee steering at her helm,
And trusts thy skill to lead her vessel through
The rocks and shoals that threaten to destroy,
And guide it to the port of happiness.
E'en now the storm that hover'd long around,
With wild appalling motion, dissipates,
And wears a rainbow at thy magic touch;
While to our anxious gaze, the sable cloud
That long has frown'd with anarchy and death,
"Turns forth its silver lining on the night,"
And mid' the shades of woe, I see a ray—
A glorious ray—the harbinger of joy!
Soon, soon the day-star of prosperity—
The glorious sun of liberty—will rise,
When all the beasts of prey and violence—
Oppressions' hated sons—will hide their heads
In every den and cave, with wild dismay.
Time was when Britain groan'd for liberty.
The dazzling sword was rais'd, and fell, and smote,
"And toss'd its twice ten thousand at a meal."
Then, nought was heard but groans, and clash of arms;
The widow's wailing, and the orphan's cries;
And where the golden harvests teem around,
Were scenes of havoc—desolated plains!
But peace to Britain now; she sheaths her sword,
And uses nobler weapons;—arguments,
Strong as the triple thunder of the foe,
Are hurl'd, and wise Minerva takes the field
Which sanguinary Mars so long has held!
Go then, brave veteran, and conquer; triumph,
With all thy noble colleagues in thy train,
Without the bloody trophy! On thy brow

Pacific laurels bloom, entwin'd with wreaths
Of olives, shrinking at the touch of blood.
Britain is glorious—is the earth's proud sun,
Which envious nations gaze at and admire!
Her glories dart athwart the wond'ring world!
Old ocean bears them on his rolling waves,
And on the pinions of the wind, they ride
To other nations and far-distant shores.
But though around the world her beams are thrown,
Upon her disc appaling spots remain!
Oh quickly heal her wrongs! to thee she cries—
To thee, her friend, to wipe away her stain;
So will she thank thee, and her sons unborn,
To latest generations, tell thy name;
The vales will echo it, and hills to hills
Repeat thee her deliverer and her friend!

On the Death of a Child.

HE is gone to his beautiful home in the skies;
   He has left these sad regions of sin;
There Jesus he views with delighted surprise,
   And with angels his pleasures begin!

Poor babe! now his sufferings for ever will cease;
   His tears and his achings are o'er;
He has found the bright regions of joy and of peace;
   He has reach'd the celestial shore!

There babes like himself with felicity crown'd,
   That beckoned his spirit while here,

Have welcom'd him home with their harps' sweetest
    As they saw his bright spirit appear.   [sound,

There Jesus himself, with ineffable love,
    Has wip'd the last tear-drop away ;
And saints, as in bands of bright glory they move,
    Have usher'd his soul into day !

O, parents ! no longer in sorrow repine ;
    'Tis Providence, gracious and wise,
Has call'd him away, that in faith you may join
    To think of your babe in the skies !

And may all at last—brothers, kindred, and friends,
    And parents, in family love,
Meet together, bright years everlasting to spend,
    In the kingdom of glory above.

Reflections.

I HAVE seen, I have seen, 'neath the azure sky
    The flow'ret in beauty array'd ;
I have heard the wind sigh, as the storm passed by ;
    And its verdure was faded—'twas dead :
And I thought, "just so frail is the glory of man ;
    "For a time he appears like the flower—
" His heart in full play, and his countenance gay,
    " When by death he's cut down in an hour !"

I have seen the cheek bloom, and the features look hale,
    And the eye sparkle gay with delight ;   [flown,
I have heard the deep moan when these beauties had
    And the eyelids were clos'd on the sight :

And I thought "like the brilliant illusions that hang
  "In the April cloud, is our life;
"Like the rainbow on high—while we flourish we die—
  "And with death wage perpetual strife!"

I have seen by the grave, the funereal train
  Passing slowly and sadly along;
I have heard the bell toll for the flight of the soul,
  And sighs from the sorrowing throng:
And I thought, as I pass'd by the home of the dead,
  "'Tis the goal that we shortly shall gain.
"There in calmness to rest on the earth's tranquil breast,
  "While the tempest beats over the plain!"

I have seen the gay Spring change to Autumn's sad tints,
  And Time hast'ning swiftly away,
And I heard—not a tread, as far onward he sped,
  Nor mortal could tempt him to stay:
And I thought "if so fleeting and fast the hours glide,
  "Each full of vexation and sorrow,
"That it surely were wise, to seize Time as he flies,
  "Nor longer indulge in to-morrow."

The Praying Sailor.

HARK! there's a voice on the midnight billow;
  A sound steals over the desolate sea;
The sailor has left his lonely pillow,
And heaves a prayer on his bended knee.

Prostrate he falls on the deck of the vessel,
As over the noiseless deep she sails,

For pardon and mercy his accents wrestle—
He's pleading with heaven, his prayer prevails.

For his friends and his country he pleads with emotion,
Though billows divide and vast seas roll between,
For he knows that the God of the land and the ocean
Is present in every place, though unseen.

No longer the dangers of shipwreck assail him,
Nor death's ghastly terrors can trouble his soul;
He knows that a Saviour's free grace cannot fail him,
Though tempest and waters wild over him roll!

Hark! there's a sound on the midnight ocean;—
The voice of the tempest is heard on the deep;
The vessel now rolls with a turbulent motion,
And high-foaming surges their barriers o'erleap!

The heavens grow blacker, the tempest increases;
Each seaman awakes, and all hands are employ'd;
But the breath of the storm tears their rigging in peices
And turbulent waters their anguish deride!

The mariners now stand, amaz'd and affrighted;
Grim Death's ghastly image confounded they view;
They remember the mercy they often have slighted,
And groans of despair burst aloud from the crew.

But this lonely sailor, his soul is resigning,
In calmness and peace, to a Saviour above;
In the anthems of heaven he soon will be joining,
Nor shipwreck nor death his fix'd spirit can move!

Hark! there's a cry on the high-rolling billow—
A sound of loud wailing is heard from the deep;

Each mariner sinks on a watery pillow—
Each rock'd by the wave in his last long sleep.

But this lonely sailor to Jesus was praying,
And smil'd as he sunk in a watery grave;
His soul for support on Jehovah was staying—
He knew his Redeemer was mighty to save!

The rest of the crew, with a wail of confusion,
Sunk dreadfully down in the vortex of death;—
Some shriek'd at their fate, and some, blind by delusion,
To the God of their spirits resigned up their breath!

Ye Christians, remote from the noise of the ocean,
Regard the poor sailor who ploughs the wild main;
Your prayers for his welfare present with devotion;
You'll find them returning in blessings again.

Spring.

THE beautiful spring flowers
 Are blooming on the lea,
And leaves and buds are opening
 On hedgerow, bush, and tree.

The merry lark above-head
 Is pouring out his joy;
He seems an atom, floating
 Betwixt the earth and sky.

The thrifty bee, 'ere sunrise,
   Goes humming on its way,
And happy-mated songsters
   Warble on every spray.

Glad voices from the meadows
   Come echoing along
Where children gather cowslips—
   A happy, healthful throng.

And many an ardent lover
   Steals forth at eventide,
To meet her in the gloaming
   He longs to make his bride.

Old age walks in the sunshine,
   With feeble tottering pace,
While graceful smiles are playing
   Upon its wrinkled face.

The rook has built his dwelling
   Along the old park wall,
In the sturdy elms that shadow
   The gray ancestral hall.

Clear sounding in the distance,
   The blackbird sings his song;
And the cuckoo's note comes stealing
   Deliciously along.

The earth is full of beauty,
   And every living thing,
In song, and joy, and gladness,
   Hails the returning Spring.

The Miller's Cottage.

(A DESCRIPTIVE SKETCH.)

BESIDE a stream, whose swiftly-flowing tide,
    A busy Mill with wat'ry stores supplied—
And as it roll'd along its winding way
Refresh'd the meads, and cheer'd the landscape gay—
There stood a cot, which to no quarry ow'd
Materials for the lowly walls it show'd;
But built of mud, with whitewash coated o'er,
An aspect rude, yet clean and decent, wore.
Upon its walls repos'd the tendril'd vine,
The clinging ivy, and bright eglantine,
Which hid them partly from the gazer's sight,
Cheq'ring the dull monotony of white.
Its front, a little garden neatly grac'd,
Where beds of herbs and flowers, arrang'd with taste,
Bespoke their owner one of cultur'd mind—
Though low in station, no illiterate hind.
Hard by, an orchard, fill'd with dusky trees,
Enrich'd the scene, and caught the passing breeze:
The laden branches, bending to the root,
In mellow autumn, hung with blushing fruit:
There grew the juicy apple; and the pear,
(Its owner's favorite), tempting, flourish'd there;
These lur'd the sight of many a passer by,
Provok'd the taste, and made young urchins sigh;
While some, more bold, would climb the alder fence
That grew around, and load themselves from thence.

Such was the miller's cottage. Honest Dan
There liv'd—a quiet and industrious man;

Few cares were mingled in his cup of life,
Save how to feed his mill, and please his wife.
His wife, to please him too, was ever bent;
Her speech was gentle, and her looks content;
Old Time had chang'd the colour of her hair,
But Dan still thought her beauty passing fair,
Lov'd her as fondly as when both were young,
And nightly listen'd to her syren tongue.
Thus on the couple lived from year to year,
In calm content, and with a conscience clear,
Each was to hospitality inclin'd:
In each, the wayfarer a friend would find,   [wind.
When faint with summer's heat, or pinch'd by winter's

My Saviour.

WHO left his shining throne on high,
    That he might suffer, bleed, and die,
To raise us rebels to the sky?
               My Saviour!

Who in a manger laid his head—
A babe within a lonely shed—
While horned oxen round him fed?
               My Saviour!

Who bore the taunts of sinful men
With meekness all his days, and when
Revil'd, revilèd not again?
               My Saviour!

Who, when the world had sunk in sleep,
Bent his tir'd course to mountains steep,
His nightly vigils there to keep?
     My Saviour!

Who for our sakes maintain'd a fight,
Singly, with hell and all its might,
And Satan's forces vanquish'd quite?
     My Saviour!

Who, in the garden, pour'd his soul
To heav'n, his sufferings to control,
While gory drops adown him roll?
     My Saviour!

Who hung upon the cross, and cried
" 'Tis finished," bow'd his head and died,
That Justice might be satisfied?
     My Saviour!

Who in the grave Death's subject lay
Until the third, th' appointed day,
Then burst its bands and rose away?
     My Saviour!

Who intercedes in heaven above,
For all who seek redeeming love,
And sends down the celestial Dove?
     My Saviour!

And shall I thy dear name deride,
And pierce afresh thy wounded side,
By cruel sins and stubborn pride?
     My Saviour!

O guide me, Jesus, lest I stray;
Lead me in Wisdom's pleasant way,

Safe to the evening of life's day,
                My Saviour!

And, when my pilgrimage shall end,
O may I, as I near the bend,
Hail thee Redeemer, Brother, Friend,
                And Saviour!

A Vision.

WILDLY romantic was the scene,
    And pensive fancies o'er me stole,
As from the towering heights of Rome,
I watch'd the last enamel'd cloud
That evening glories pencil'd. Bright
Its burning form with sapphire flam'd,
As through the azure skies it sail'd
Into the glowing west, to guard
The charioteer of heaven, and catch
His ling'ring farewell rays. Awhile
It floated there, and smiling, kiss'd
The mossy tow'rs, and mould'ring fanes
By which I was surrounded; then
Its beauty was reflected back
By Tiber's dark and silent stream,
Which in a vale beneath my feet
Majestically roll'd.
                But soon
Night's shadows stole its crimson hue,
And chang'd its rosy tints to those
Of deepest violet, and more dark

It still became, until the moon,
Wheel'd her fair course along the heavens—
When it was seen no longer.
    Silence,
With gloom and night, then held their reign
Unbroken, save by dolorous screams
Of owlets in their dim abodes,
Or fragments, which at intervals
Broke from the crumbling stones, and roll'd
With a faint, dreary echo down!
Or, by wild cat'racts, rudely form'd
By broken arches, which in pride
Once rear'd their giant concaves o'er
The wid'ning flood, but now o'erthrown
By all-consuming Time, they form'd
A pond'rous bed, o'er which the stream
Confusedly flow'd on, and flung
A lonely noise on all around.

 Alone I mus'd amid the gloom,
And saw the moon with placid beam,
Romantic, tip the ruinous scene,
And bathe in her pure silv'ry light,
Turret and mould'ring column. Long
I wander'd mid' these wrecks of time—
Of ages hoar fled long ago—
And gaz'd upon the broken shapes
Of monumental arches; rude
They stretch'd their horned peaks afar
Into the night, like horrid tusks
Of fabled monsters, dire and dread—
Silent mementoes of the past!
No bell announc'd the flight of time,

But the fair empress of the night
Had risen to her zenith, while
A deep and solemn stillness told
To all with more than oral sounds
It was the hour of midnight.   Gloom,
Reigning all around, now held
The breath of Æolus; no wind
Shook the lone thistle on the walls,
Or swept in dreary gusts adown
The mould'ring avenue; but still,
Methought at this dread hour, I heard
Strange sounds and weird noises, sweep
Along the gloomy ruins; yet
The silv'ry grass that crown'd their tops
Bent not nor wav'd!

       An ancient tower
Now caught mine eye, on whose gray sides
The moon-beams fell, and to me show'd,
Or seem'd to show, a ghostly form,
That rose from its dark shades, and grew
Still more distinct and human!
Gauntly the spectre wav'd its hand,
And with a silent footstep mov'd
From the gray turret, whence it rose
Nearer and nearer, till it reach'd
The open terrace where I stood!
I would have fled, but some weird spell
Enchain'd my limbs and fix'd my sight
Upon the phantom, which advanc'd,
And, bending o'er a broken column,
Tore the dank nightshade from its sides,
As thus it spake :—

"O tim'rous mortal!
"Why dost thou tremble at my spectral form?
"I came not to appall thee, but to show
"To thee the vanity of earthly things.
"Behold yon silv'ry moon; mark how she rides
"Along the pathless blue, and scatters down
"Her tranquil beams o'er these fantastic ruins:
"But a few cent'ries since, her beams here shone
"Not on a waste, but on a famous city:
"Where is this famous city? where is she
"Who sway'd her sceptre o'er the cringing nations,
"While on yon mount, deserted now, but then
"Throng'd by the great and wise, I sat at eve
"And sung her pomp and splendour? yes, I sung them,
"For I am Horace; yet ah! where is now
"Imperial Rome, the theme of Horace' song?
"And thus it must be, yes, and Britain's pride—
"She who now sits arrayed in pomp and glory,
"And whose fair name the rolling ocean bears—
"Must bow to Time's inexorable hand,
"And ghostly shadows stalk amid those scenes
"That now resound with gaiety and life!
"But there are realms above the glitt'ring stars,
"Where ruin never enters, there lay up
"Thy choicest treasures, for these desert wastes
"With the sad voice of desolation, tell
"Terrestrial pomp is fleeting!"

  The phantom vanish'd; but I heard
  Again the accents of his words
  In every crumbling fragment, while
  The rolling waters at my feet,
  As on they rippled, seem'd to say
  "Terrestrial pomp is fleeting!"

Patrons.

The Right Hon. the Lord Bishop of Peterborough; His Grace the Duke of Buccleuch; The Right Hon. Lord Brougham; The Right Hon. Earl Spencer; The Right Hon. Lord Lgveden; Sir Fitzroy Kelly, Q.C., M.P.; The Rev. Lord Alwyne Compton; Lord Walter Scott; Lord Burghley, M.P.; G. W. Hunt, Esq., M.P.; P. A. Taylor, Esq., M.P.; The Hon. and Rev. D. Finch Hatton; Lady P. P. Duncombe; Captain Maunsell Tibbitts; H. O. Nethercote, Esq.; Thos. Carlyle, Esq.; J. E. Ryland, Esq., M.A.; &c., &c.

List of Subscribers.

Abull, Mr. W., Wellingborough
Adams, Mr. J. W., Kettering
Allen, Mr. W., Kettering
Askham, Mr. J., Wellingborough

Baker, Mr. Joseph, Kettering
Bamford, Mr. Geo., Rushton
Bartlett, Mrs., Burton Lattimer Rectory
Bates, Mr. Geo., Kettering
Beadman, Mr., Rushton
Bellamy, Mr. B., Wellingborough
Biddles, Mr., Kettering
Bigge, Rev. H. J., Rockingham
Bourne, Mr. Alfred A., Windmill St., Gravesend.
Brown, Mr. S. R., Kettering
Browne, Rev. A. W., Gretton
Brougham, Right Hon. Lord
Bryant, Mr. W., Wellingborough
Buccleuch, His grace the Duke of (5 copies)
Buckby, Mr. W., Kettering
Burghley, Lord, M.P.
Butterfield, J., Esq., *Herald* Office, Northampton

Carlyle, Thos., Esq., Chelsea
Carr, Rev. T., Loddington
Chappell, Mr. T., Leicester
Clayton, Rev. T., Cottingham
Chettle, Mr. R., Kettering
Cocker, Mr., Kettering
Compton, Rev. Lord Alwyne, Castle Ashby
Corby, Mr. G., Northampton
Cornwell, Rev. T. C. B., Geddington
Cox, Mr. Geo., Middleton
Cox, Mr. C. H., Bridge Street, Northampton
Cox, Mr. W., Northampton
Curtis, Mr. Thos., Wellingborough

Dale, Mr. W., Barton Seagrave Lodge
Dash, Mr. W., Kettering
De Wilde, G. J., Esq., *Mercury* Office, Northampton
Drage, Mr., 84, Connaught Terrace, London (2 copies)
Drakeford, Rev. S., Desborough
Draper, Mr. H., Royal Hotel, Kettering
Dryden, Sir H. L., Bart.
Dryland, J. W., Esq., Kettering
Dulley, Mr. W., Wellingborough
Duncombe, Lady P. P.

East, Mr. Chas., Kettering
Eland, G., Esq., Thrapston (2 copies)
Eldred, Mr. Geo., Kettering
Ellis, F., Esq., County Court Judge
Elwes, Val. Carey, Esq., Desborough Hall
Emery, Mr. T., Leicester
Etheridge, Rev. S., Kettering
Euston, Earl of, M.P.
Exton, Rev. W., Kettering

Farey, Mr. W., Kettering
Farey, Mr. Samuel, Shipton, Yorkshire
Field, Mr. G., Barton Seagrave
Fisher, Geo., Esq., Market Harborough

Flavel, Mr., Kettering
Forster, John, Esq., Barrister at Law, London
Franklin, Mr., Barford Lodge
Friends at Kettering and elsewhere (10 copies)

Garrard, W., Esq., Kettering
Gedge, Rev. Sidney, Vicar of All Saint's, Northampton.
Gibbins, Mr. Henry, Peacock Inn, Kettering
Gibbon, W., Esq.
Gibbon, Rev. Chas., Lutton
Gibbon, James, Esq., Kettering
Ginns, Mr. Joseph, Rothwell
Goode, Mr. Joseph, Kettering
Goodfellow, Mr. James, Kettering
Goodfellow, Mr. F., Kettering
Goosey, John, Esq., Kettering
Gue, Mr. P. M., Rothwell

Hafford, Mr. C., Rothwell
Harradine, Mr. Thomas, George Hotel, Kettering
Hanger, Mr. Henry, Kettering
Hatton, Hon. and Rev. D Finch, Weldon Rectory
Heighton, Mr. Henry, Kettering
Henson, Mr. W., Kettering
Heycock, Rev. C., Pytchley
Hickling, Rev. E. L., Halesworth, Suffolk
Hircock, Mr. W., Kettering
Hobson, James, Esq., Isham
Hogg, Rev. Lewis, Castle Sanderson (2 copies)
Horne, Mr. S., Kettering
Hopkins, Mr. John, Dr. Mark's Orchestra, Jersey
Humphries, Mr. W., Wellingborough
Hunnybun, Rev. James., Kettering
Hunt, G. W., Esq., M.P. (2 copies)

Isham, Rev. R., Lamport

James, Rev. T., Theddingworth
Jeffries, Mr., Kettering
Jeffries, Mr. L., 4, Crescent Place, Norwich

Kelley, Sir Fitzroy, Q.C., M.P. (12 copies)

Lamb, Mrs., Kettering
Lamb, G. W., Esq., Kettering
Lammie, Mr., Kettering
Lancum, Mr. J. Warkton
Law, E. F., Esq., Northampton
Lea, Rev. Joseph, Moulton, (2 copies)
Leigh, Mr. Arthur L., Northampton
Lewis, Rev. Evan, B.A., F.G.S., Rothwell
Loasby, Mr. Joseph, Kettering
Loftus, Mr., Kettering
Logan, J., Esq., M.D., Kettering
Lyvedon, Right Hon. Lord
Madge, Rev. T. H., Kettering
Maddocks, Mr. E., Kettering
Malivoise, Mr. J., Kettering
Margetts, Mr. J., builder, Kettering
Matthews, Mrs.
Maunsell, Rev. G. E., Thorpe Malsor (2 copies)
McLoskey, P. Esq., M.D., Rothwell (3 copies)
Mence, Rev. R., Carlton
Morton, Rev. R., Rothwell
Murphy, W. Esq., Wellingborough
Mursell, Rev. J., Kettering

Naylor, Mr., Kettering
Nethercote, H. O., Esq., Moulton Grange (3 copies)
Newman, Mr., Cranford
Nicholson, Rev. G., Northampton
Norwood, Mr. W., Kettering

Osborne, Mr. James, Kettering

Pain, P., Esq., Boughton House, Kettering
Pain, Rev. P., Boughton
Palmer, Geoffry, Esq., Carlton
Paybody, Mrs., Kettering
Pearson, Colonel, Oakley Hall
Peel, Mr., Barton Seagrave (2 copies)

Peterborough, Right Rev. Bishop of (6 copies)
Plummer, Mr. J., Kettering (2 copies)
Phipps, Pickering, Esq., Northampton
Phipps, J. Esq., Mayor of Northampton
Porch, Mr. John, Kettering
Pulver, Mr. T., Broughton

Rains, Mr. Joseph, Kettering
Reynolds, Mr. W., Leicester
Riley, B. Esq., Desborough
Rollins, Miss Ann, Gravesend (2 copies)
Rotton, R., Esq., Brompton, London (3 copies)
Roughton, J. J., Esq., Kettering
Roughton, Rev. W. C., Great Harrowden Vicarage
Rowlatt, Mr. Charles, Kettering
Rubbra, Mr., Gravesend
Rubbra, W. A., Esq., Wellingborough
Rutherford, Mr. J., Northampton (2 copies)
Ryland, J. E., Esq., M.A., Northampton

Salmon, Mr. Thomas, Kettering
Scott, Lord Walter (2 copies)
Sibley, Mr. Samuel, Kettering
Simpkinson, Rev. J. M., Brington
Soulter, Mrs., Tunbridge Wells
Spencer, Right Hon. Earl
Stiles, Mr. James, Rushton
Stockburn, Joseph, Esq., Kettering
Stockburn, J. T., Esq., Kettering
Stopford, Rev. G. P., Warkton
Sturgess, Mr. W., Kettering
Sutton, the Misses, Weekly Cottage (4 copies)
Sutton, Rev. J. L., Weekly (2 copies)

Taylor, Mr., Thapstone (2 copies)
Taylor, P. A. Esq., M.P., London.
Tayleur, Mr. S., Rothwell
Taylor, Mr. W., Bishopgate Street, London
Tearnby, — Esq., the Grove, Gravesend

Tearle, Rev. F., Kettering (2 copies)
Tibbitts, B. Maunsell, Esq., Barton Seagrave (2 copies
Tingle, Mr. John, Kettering
Timpson, Mr. Charles, Manchester
Toller, W., Esq., Kettering
Toller, Mr. J., Kettering
Towndrow, Mr., Kettering

Waddington, Mr. Thomas, junior, Kettering
Waddington, Mr. Richard, Kettering
Wall, Mr. James, Kettering
Wallis, Mr. John, Kettering
Watkins, Rev., F. C., Brixworth
Wells, Mr. Joseph, Kettering
Weston, Mr. Enoch, Northampton
Whitmore, Mr. W., Leicester
Wignell, Mr., Burton Lattimer
Willis, Mrs. Jonathan, Kettering
Wilmott, Rev. A., Bearswood
Wright, Mr. A., Kettering
Wrigley, Mr. James, Kettering
Wrigley, Mr. F., Hawarden, Chester
Wyse, Mr., Weekly

Yeomans, Mr. G., Desborough

www.ingramcontent.com/pod-product-compliance
Lightning Source LLC
Chambersburg PA
CBHW080435110426
42743CB00016B/3174